Quakers in Scotland

An anthology of the thoughts and
activities of the Religious Society of
Friends past and present

Acknowledgements

ISBN 0 9514971 0 3

Designed and Typeset
by *Curlew Graphics*, Yetholm, Kelso, TD5 8PD

Printed and Bound in Kelso for the publishers

The Religious Society of Friends, Scotland,
c/o 8 Myrtle Park, Glasgow, G42 8UQ

Cover Illustration by Anne Woolgrove

We are indebted to Edward Milligan for his help and encouragement in this project, and to the Edith M. Ellis Trust for financial assistance. Our special thanks to Anne Woolgrove for her research into Celtic art and subsequent detailed drawings. We are grateful too, to all those who sent us contributions, regardless of whether we have been able to include them.

In addition to those Friends whose contributions are attributed, we wish to thank many more without whose help and interest this book would not have been possible. These include William Aitken, Anne Benzie, Jill Blackadder, June Braithwaite, Peter Christy, Anne Cook, Mary Dower, Nigel Dower, Andrew Farrar, Friends House Library Staff, Stanley Johnson, Muriel Lloyd-Pritchard, Pippa Ludlam, Tom Macdonald, Sandy McEwan, Alastair McIntosh, Delia Seager, Nancy Selkirk, Avis Swarbrick, Fran Woolgrove, James Woolgrove and Margaret Woolgrove. We shall, inevitably have forgotten some who have contributed to the exercise - our thanks to them are no less sincere.

We have sought permission to reproduce copyright material and record our thanks to all those who have given consent. We apologise if through oversight we have inadvertently reproduced any copyright material without permission.

Philip Bryers
Nicola Maharg
Jenny Neilson
David Woolgrove
July 1989

CONTENTS

Introduction

Fàilte do'n Alba *Welcome to Scotland!*

London Yearly Meeting in Aberdeen in 1989 promises to be an occasion to remember. Friends in Scotland are delighted to welcome so many visiting Friends - not just from other parts of London Yearly Meeting, but from Yearly Meetings throughout the world. We trust that everyone will leave with warm memories, and as part of our "guid Scots welcome", the idea of this publication was conceived. It is intended to give a flavour of Quakerism north of the border - past and present.

When London Yearly Meeting first met in Scotland, in 1948, a more weighty publication appeared. William H. Marwick, MA, then Clerk of Scotland General Meeting, wrote *A Short History of Friends in Scotland,* from which we have drawn, with appreciation, in the section of this publication containing historical material. For good measure, William Marwick added a "Life and Appreciation of Robert Barclay, 1648-1690 and a Précis of the Apology for the True Christian Divinity."

Our purpose is less erudite, but we hope we shall inform and stimulate as well as entertain. The process of pulling together our material has been most pleasurable, and we have become particularly conscious of two themes. The first is well illustrated by an anecdote which was passed to us:

"Several years ago I regularly visited an old lady who lived in the top flat of a tenement in Gorgie (Edinburgh) on her own. After several visits, she asked me, in her North East Scotland accent, 'Wad ye mind telling me which kirk you come frae?' 'I'm a Quaker.' Silence for a while, then, 'My, my, I thocht they were a' deid'"

To counteract any such suspicions we have balanced our brief venture into the past with some contemporary pieces reflecting Scottish Friends today.

Second, we became aware as we sifted through all the contributions we received for consideration, that many of us have the good fortune to live in comfort in some of the most beautiful parts of Scotland. Is that the whole story of Scottish Friends today? We hope not, and to emphasise the less attractive realities of life in parts of urban Scotland we have tried to draw upon examples of Quaker life and witness in these places too.

We hope you like the end result, and we conclude with the old Scots saying:

"Haste Ye Back!"

Friends travelling from south of the border to Aberdeen for the first time will realise that Scotland is a big country - and there is plenty more to the north and west of Aberdeen. It's another 200 miles to Thurso by road or rail, and the best part of a day's journey to Orkney, Shetland, Uist or Lewis, on each of which there are Friends. There are sizeable Preparative Meetings in Scotland, for example Edinburgh Central (125 adult members) and Glasgow (95), but most of the remaining 400 or so members are well scattered; of the 23 Preparative Meetings and Recognised Meetings, 15 are made up of less than 20 members. Even the large total membership for Glasgow is misleading because remote members on the islands tend to be associated with Glasgow Preparative Meeting rather than their nearest (but still very distant) mainland meeting.

This 'diasporic' nature of Scottish Friends means that they have certain unique characteristics. For example, there are few inactive members in Scotland because it is hard to hide in a group of ten. Scottish Quakers must also be seasoned travellers, as the venues for General Meeting and Monthly Meetings rotate regularly. In addition to these formal visits, many Friends from the larger meetings see it as an enjoyable duty to visit the outlying

5

small meetings during holidays and at other times. There is a network of arrangements and financial assistance to ensure that isolated young Friends are involved in the life of the Society. All of these factors serve to bind Friends in Scotland into a close grouping with a well-defined identity.

It is not unknown for Friends House to ask for an 11 am meeting to be arranged in Orkney for a visiting speaker, to be followed by lunch in Oban and a 6.30pm slide show at Castle Douglas! We hope that Yearly Meeting in Aberdeen will serve to dispel such geographical uncertainties, and that in future we might have our visitors for a little longer!

Bob Hay (Ayr Meeting)

An examination of the General Meeting for Scotland Books of Members for 1921, 1949 and 1989, yields further interesting information. Only one meeting - Aberdeen - still meets in the same Meeting House as it did in 1921. Indeed, of the 13 places supporting a meeting in 1921, only Aberdeen, Dundee,

Edinburgh and Glasgow continue to do so.

Between 1921 and 1948, membership of the Society in Scotland grew by around 40 to just

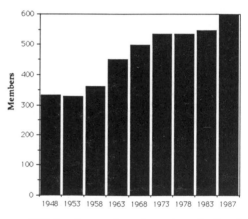

Data from "YM Tab. Statements "

over 300, but the number of meetings declined from 13 to 9. Since 1949, membership has nearly doubled and meetings have started in about 20 new locations throughout Scotland.

It is salutary to set Quakers in a wider religious context. We have around 600 members and we own only 6 Meeting Houses in Scotland. In comparison, there are 823,000 adult members of the Church of Scotland, 282,000 Roman Catholics, 24,400 Muslims, 12,900 Mormons, 10,000 Hindus and 10,000 Sikhs, and 5,000 adult members of the Salvation Army. The Church of Scotland has a massive 1,740 congregations or parishes, and it is estimated that there are between 100 and 200 house churches in Scotland. Seen in this light, we might be described as insignificant, though it is hoped that in reality we are not.

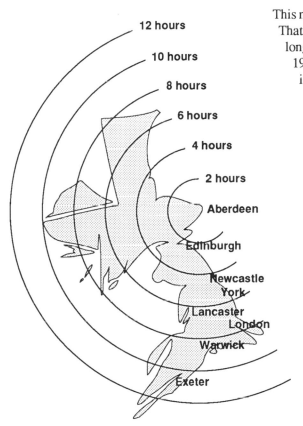

12 hours
10 hours
8 hours
6 hours
4 hours
2 hours
Aberdeen
Edinburgh
Newcastle
York
Lancaster
London
Warwick
Exeter

This map is drawn on an equi-temporal scale. That is, places are plotted according to how long it takes to travel to Aberdeen using the 1988-89 British Rail Timetable. Curves indicate the number of hours it takes to travel to Aberdeen. Places marked are those of earlier residential Yearly Meetings together with London and Edinburgh for reference. There are inconsistencies in the map due to the differences in journey time on the East and West Coast Main Lines and due to the BR network.

Andrew Farrar

Moving to Scotland

Moving to Scotland in October 1988 was a big decision for us, but Michael and I felt that the way of life and the beautiful surroundings would more than compensate for coming so far north of friends and family. Michael is a professional gardener with nearly 40 years' experience and I am a gardener by nature who has kept our family in fruit and vegetables for most of our married life. Here we have for the first time the opportunity to be able to work together at something we both love doing. We moved here with Helen, our middle daughter, who as a landscape architecture student, takes a keen interest in our surroundings (and drew the two pictures).

We have come to care for a walled kitchen garden in a small country estate in the Tweed valley. The property belongs to Mr. Jeremy Bates and has been in his family for over 400 years. He married an English Friend, Elizabeth Rudd, and they have 2 young children. They have a great feeling of responsibility for their heritage and we feel a very special atmosphere here. The grounds are semi-wild and a wonderful place for the children and animals. The house is a friendly, comfortable family home and we enjoy being part of their extended family.

The Borders is full of country houses with their accompanying farms, parkland, gate lodges and, usually, a walled kitchen garden. Anton's Hill is one of the very few where the walled garden is still used as it was originally intended. Rather overgrown, as it had been 2 years since the previous devoted gardener left, it still contained box hedges, trained fruit trees, frames, beds and borders; with a 100 year old vine and a splendid wall of geraniums in the greenhouse. We have tried in vain to find similar gardens in this area. Many have become Garden Centres or commercial nurseries, some are tree plantations or just rough grass, some contain tennis courts or swimming pools, and one or two are now small housing estates.

We are trying very hard to keep the garden much as it was, so that it will be there to hand on to the next generation. It is extremely well placed and layed out, sloping to the south with a fine view of the Cheviots and sheltered to the north-east by an enormous stand of tall trees. The walls of hedges offer protection from the almost continuous winds and the sun streams in and is caught by the high walls. Working in the garden is like being in a different world. There is no electricity so in mid-winter work is only possible between 8.30 am and 3.30 pm, but as spring advances we are soon able to spend longer and longer in the garden and greenhouse. We try to use traditional methods where suitable, and Michael is delighted to be doing things that he was told about by old gardeners from private service with whom he worked as an apprentice.

Our present house is a tiny gate lodge, low and snug when the winds roar in the treetops. Eventually we shall move into the gardener's cottage right by the walled garden, which will be much more convenient for work, but being well inside the grounds, would not have been so handy for getting to know the neighbours!

We have found local people extremely helpful

and friendly. On the phone or in the shops "It's no problem" is a well used phrase and sums up the attitude. In the village we have to listen very carefully to understand the accent.

I tended to forget at first that I could speak *my* language (English) and be completely understood even though I was having difficulty understanding theirs. Life is slower here than we were used to, but none the worse for that. Local meetings are held in a more relaxed and causal way, yet just as much business is accomplished. A cheery 'Hello' is more usual than a formal handshake.

We have moved to a village similar in size to the one we left in Worcestershire and our life-style here is very similar, but the sudden dropping of all the responsibilities that I had accumulated over the years has made this seem like a holiday. Having been PM clerk, the change to being a newcomer in a small recognised Meeting has been very relaxing. The same happened with the W.I., which as secretary or president I had helped to run for many years. Coming to Scotland and the 'Rural' I am very happy to be simply a member. I have been encouraged to join the local Church of Scotland Women's Guild and was amused to be told there of all the Quakers who live in this area.

After a few months experience of living in the Borders, with its very sparce population and beautiful sunrises, the proximity to both the sea and the hills, the fresh opportunities for work in garden, village and Meeting, I am very glad that we came.

Alison Tyas

Living in the Borders

Observant Friends will have noticed the imprint "Curlew Graphics" on the Christmas appeal from Friends House and on the financial leaflet issued in the Spring, as well as on some Q.P.S. publications. Here is the story behind Curlew Graphics...and this book, which would not have been possible without the enterprise and enthusiasm of David Woolgrove and his family.

We moved to Yetholm in the Borders from Oban in the autumn of 1987 into an old farm house dating back some 200 years. Our nearest neighbours are just under a mile away and the village of Yetholm itself is about 2 miles distant.

We had lived in Oban for eight years and were increasingly feeling that we were out on a limb. We all wanted to take a more active role within the Society, but because of distance, we found this rather difficult. In spite of our flurry of activity in the summer months, the autumn, winter and spring months left us with very little contact with the wider family of Friends.

We had looked at alternative places in which to live, so that when the opportunity arose for David to take early retirement, we seized it very quickly. We chose the Borders because of its ease of access. It is only about 4 hours away from London by train, about an hour from Edinburgh, 2 hours from Glasgow and within easy access to the whole of Scotland and the North of England. It was an extra bonus that the people in the Borders have proved to be extremely friendly and very hospitable.

Earlston Meeting in the Borders was held in a Friend's home. Meeting was held on two Sundays a month. In the new year, the group started meeting weekly and it became clear in the summer of 1988 that the Meeting was beginning to outgrow the accommodation at Earlston. We started having Meeting in people's homes and a map was drawn marking the location of every family in order to find the most central point for a regular Meeting. Kelso was selected and we eventually settled in the Community Education centre in the old Abbey Row School buildings in the town. The room we have for Meeting for Worship looks out to Kelso Abbey, which dates back many centuries. Every Sunday there are on average around 15-20 Friends and attenders who meet regularly. Sometimes our Meeting swells to just under 30. Another group of Borders Friends meets in Peebles and Innerleithen.

11

Yetholm Loch

Being liberated from the hassle of the education system after 20 years or more was a wonderful experience, but it isn't possible to live without gainful employment. It seemed very obvious to us that we should build upon our educational experience, which had included writing modules for classroom use and designing work packs for pupils. Consequently, when we were considering what we would do to earn a living, we built upon these sound foundations to develop Curlew Graphics, a desktop publishing business. This involves us in graphic design and typography for the production of books, textbooks, leaflets, and more mundane things such as letterheads and business cards. We are trying to do as much work as possible for the Society of Friends in this field since we particularly enjoy putting our skills and our equipment to their service. Apart from the graphic design and typography side of the business, we are developing two very exciting educational projects which we hope will be of great service to schools throughout Britain. Developing a business from scratch is not an easy task, but it is certainly a challenge!

David & Fran Woolgrove.

One exciting thing to have happened in 1989 is that Friends in the Borders put forward a minute to the Monthly Meeting requesting that their status of Recognised Meeting be changed to that of a Preparative Meeting. We are now able to report that Borders Meeting is officially a Preparative Meeting.

12

FRIENDS IN SCOTLAND IN 1986

In June 1986, Christine Davis, Clerk of General Meeting for Scotland, wrote to Clerks and Correspondents in Scotland advising that the main theme for residential General Meeting in September 1986 was to be the state of the Society in Scotland. She quoted the query, first asked by Yearly Meeting in 1682: "How has the Truth prospered amongst you, and how are Friends in Peace and Unity?"

We quote selectively from the reports and minutes received from 27 meetings - or groups or families of Friends - throughout the country:

"We...meet once a month in each other's homes for worship, a shared lunch, and a Meeting for learning - and this has deepened our understanding of what we believe. ...A small group of those members who are free to attend meets fortnightly midweek to pray for peace and for those in the Third World. Small meetings such as our own, although scattered in distance, reach a closeness in unity and in friendship that makes for a loving Fellowship."
(Dumfries & Galloway)

"Within its small compass the Meeting embraces an extraordinary diversity of human types. We have developed a loving tolerance and understanding of one another's concerns and habits, in spite of our differences... We have at times found ourselves caught up in deep discussion of matters concerning our spiritual lives."
(Glasgow Wednesday Evening Meeting)

"Ministry is not frequent in our Meetings for Worship, but we have few completely silent meetings. We believe the ministry is sufficient: it is accepted and acceptable. We talk and listen to each other after all our meetings and sometimes between them... We are conscious of a failure in outreach. We try. Sustain us with your prayers and perhaps the occasional visit.
(East Kilbride)

"In the last few years Ayr Meeting has changed from being a small elderly Allowed Meeting with no children, which held Meeting for Worship once a month, to being a Preparative Meeting which meets each week, with several

13

young families and a regular children's group. An average attendance may be 10 or 12, but a good attendance would be 20 adults and 5 children. This contrasts with the five or six Friends who used to meet. However, it is due to the constancy and faith of that small group that the Meeting is thriving today." (Ayr)

"It is an exciting time. We feel that the Truth is working in us as a leaven, and we shall try to help it prosper. There is a growing feeling of unity among us, as we recognise newcomers and they recognise us too as fellow seekers.

"Our unity has not been tested, however. We have not yet faced, as a Meeting, any of those issues which divide the world. Our members' concerns are not yet obvious because they are not shared with the Meeting. Until recently our Meetings for Worship were largely silent, and as a recognised Meeting we had few business meetings. Concerns have therefore tended to be shared with a few like-minded members or in outside organisations. This may change."

(Inverness)

"Whenever there is a study group or conference, the amount and quality of the ministry goes up. However, many of us do not make enough time during the week for what some call prayer, meditation or time for 'being' rather than 'doing'. We do not come with heart and mind sufficiently prepared. We expect too much of the silence and sometimes our Meetings are shallow."

(Aberdeen)

"One of our greatest joys has been the number of our children and young people who have grown up among us and became absolutely central to the life of the Meeting. This has meant a lot of work all year round by those responsible for organising Sunday morning activities, weekend camps, outings and so on, but it always seems to have been time and effort unstintingly given and the reward lies in seeing a group of young people going off every few years taking with them, we hope, a Foundation of Quaker values for future spiritual experience.

"An experiment which has become part of our regular worship is what we call 'Family worship,' a Meeting for Worship in which the young people share with us a more structured form of worship, with contributions in music, readings and ministry. We have also had our young people as doorkeepers on occasion. Recently we returned to holding 'readings meetings' half an hour before Meeting for Worship once a month, to help us prepare in mind and heart."

(St. Andrews)

"There are...difficulties which we certainly share with other Meetings - patchy attendance at business meetings, an imbalance of women to men in the Meeting, a high proportion of members whose partners are not in membership, an overburdening of some with jobs that require to be done. In recognising these as areas which we need to address, we also recognise that we do not openly share these difficulties with other Meetings and that we know very little of how other Meetings deal with them."

(St. Andrews)

"We recognise that we have only an indistinct and perhaps inadequate idea of the detail of each other's beliefs. What we appear to share in unity is our quest for truth and meaning."

(Edinburgh, Stafford Street)

"Truth has prospered in our Meeting during the last year, with a growth spiritually and numerically in evidence. To continue with this growth we need both to share our search for Truth in study groups or similar gatherings and to join more fully in the life of our Monthly Meetings and the Society as a whole."

(Polmont)

Minute 13 of General Meeting for Scotland, 20-21 September, 1986 reads:
"We need to learn from one another, know one another face to face, before we can begin to reach out to others, for our religious life is arid if it is cut off from the world of which we are inescapably a part. We must continue to question what it is that we believe, and how our beliefs relate to our actions.

15

A Meeting of Friends at Polmont

"If the truth is indeed working in us as a leavener, these questions will not go away, but will require our continuing attention as we meet for worship, for study, for celebration, in social gatherings and over informal meals, sharing our laughter and our tears and in all these ways coming to know one another in the things which are eternal."

In the unuttered silence of the circle
My body moves cautiously
Not too often in the hour.

Within
Thoughts, images, sensations
Pour through a thousand breaches
And drown the cultivated void
In deafening turmoil.

Does clay moan inwardly
Mute in the potter's hands?
Is iron in torment as it flows
Incandescently
Into the waiting mould?
Does worked silver scream
Beyond the pitch of hearing
During the long drawn out transformation
From plain ingot to intricate filigree?

As raw material
I am accepted whole by my Creator
As finished article
I am fit only for meltdown
Or return to the ceaseless wheel.

And yet I marvel at the perfection
Of familiar faces
Glimpsed in a brief outflowing moment
Facing me
Eyes closed or downcast
On the carpet's infinite distance underfoot.

I hold them precious
In my stilling mind.

Neil Mochrie

CDEETING FOR WORSHIP IN SHETLAND

Duncan Blackadder from Scalloway gives us a 12 year old's view of going to Meeting in the Shetlands.

One thing I like about going to meeting in Shetland is that you go to lots of different people's houses. Sometimes we go to this peerie* chapel beside Helen and Tom's but that's not very often.

Best of all is Jenni's house*[at Walls]*. She lives in a croft house with one room. She has a spinning wheel and a box bed, a braaly[†] old cooking stove with lots of doors in it. She has a long wooden seat with sheepskins and her window sills are full of flower pots. You can see the sea very near and you can hear it and hear the wind and sea gulls and goats.

Next best is Whalsay where the Dallys live because we get to go there on two long ferry crossings and you can watch sea-birds and islands and cliffs. You can see all the houses in Symbister from their house and the new Leisure Centre is being built next door. In 1992 we might be able to go swimming because that's when the pool is supposed to be finished.

After Whalsay I like Unst best because we get to go on four ferries and I can sometimes go on the bridge. Last time I went on the bridge we saw a cargo ship and we had to alter course. The crew looked through my binoculars and said that they were better than the skipper's ones. His had only one eye piece working.

I like meeting in our own house because you don't have to go anywhere and you can make tea and things for other people. I like it best when Rachel comes with her two children even if they are peerie. It was good when the American children came last year and I could show them my room.

Helen and Tom have a big house *[at Tresta]* and they have toys for children who come. Tom let me print on his computer and we asked each other questions on the computer.

Derek's house *[at Lerwick]* is full of pictures and he has stuffed birds. Last time we heard a record from Russia with Russian bird song on it. You can watch birds from his window.

I liked Pat Justad's house for meeting. It was good fun because I could play with Peerie Tor.

17

They lived in the north mainland and it was good when we had time to walk along the volcanic cliffs by the lighthouse, but Pat has moved south now.

I haven't been to the Jacobsen's house *[on Bressay]* for a meeting yet or to any other Shetland Quaker families' houses but I would like to some time.

I just wish that there were more children in the Quaker families up here, so I like it when we go south and go to Aberdeen or Saffron Walden Meetings because I can meet lots more children like Bijon and Rudi. But I still feel glad that I live in Shetland.

*Peerie: Small, tiny, wee (Shetland word)
†Braaly: Good, splendid, excellent (Shetland form of bravo)

Shetland Islands

VICTORIA TERRACE, EDINBURGH

Scotland's newest Meeting House is that recently acquired by S.E. Scotland Monthly Meeting for Central Edinburgh Meeting, just off the Royal Mile. After the arduous tasks of fund raising and restoration, Friends took up occupancy in late 1988. Here Ian Ramsey, one of the Meeting House wardens, writes about some of their plans for the future.

Edinburgh's new Meeting House is situated on the corner of Victoria Terrace and the Upper Bow. It was finally occupied by Friends in October 1988 after two years of rebuilding. Originally it was constructed in 1865 as a chapel for a group that seceded from the Church of Scotland in the mid 18th C. In 1965 the Boys Brigade used the building as their local headquarters. Stafford Street Friends in their search for premises were attracted by the spacious aspect of the building and by its central location. The financial burden of moving has almost been overcome now with generous assistance from charitable funds and with great efforts by members.

The building has three storeys. The Meeting Room is on the top floor with windows overlooking the old town and all the way to the Pentland Hills. The sun shines in all day long. The meeting room, which seats 150, at last allows us to sit in circles and to see each other.

The floor below has another large hall and is used by the older children. Leading off from this are the library, kitchen and creche. Recently a stained glass window was fitted in the library to commemorate our Friend John Selkirk, who died in 1988.

The ground floor has a foyer and windows suitable for displays. Midweek Meetings are occasionally held in the foyer and provide pedestrians with their first glimpse of Quakerism - it reminds us of the Native Americans observing Friends at worship in Pennsylvania!

In a wing off the foyer is the Warden's office and a 'community' office let out on a time-share basis to an ecumenical AIDS group called Positive Help. These rooms also have shop windows and a door directly onto the small street called Upper Bow. Although the walls of the Meeting House are rather bare at present, moves are afoot to fix notice boards. A workshop group is organising an Amish style tapestry to fill some of the larger spaces.

Whilst the work was being carried out, the Meeting met in Gilles College, a Roman Catholic seminary and at St. Marks Unitarian Church,

19

thereby enhancing our ecumenical links. Various interest groups met in Friends' houses. This meant that Friends got to know each other better, and although most groups have now moved back to the Meeting House, some Friends are keen not to lose the strengths and experiences found in each others' homes during the 'exile'.

In the seven months since our return we have begun to host various initiatives of a spiritual and community nature. Use in connection with the Justice, Peace and Integrity of Creation (JPIC) exercise and use by the Church of Scotland during its General Assembly means we are playing a full part in the network of local church groups.

Other regular users are Amnesty, Christian CND, Housing groups and associations, the Scottish Association for the Care and Resettlement of Offenders (SACRO), adoption and fostering groups, Esperantists and the resident AIDS project, Positive Help, which trains volunteers here. Various Buddhist groups are also hoping to come. An interesting tradi-

tional dance group which research ancient and nearly forgotten Scottish dances and then re-create them meets weekly in the hall. Friends of the Earth and the Green Party hope to use the premises. The Meeting is pleased to assist these growing points in the community. Friends are deeply involved with many of the above groups but the Meeting is also adapting to being settled again by developing various fellowships where personal growth and development can be fostered in an atmosphere of tolerance and acceptance. A new idea which arose from some ministry is that we need a separate forum where concerns can be shared with others in the Meeting. The topic of the first forum is the loss of the tropical rainforests and the threats not only to indigenous native peoples, flora and fauna but also to global weather patterns. Local and Regional Councillors and journalists as well as local groups are to be invited to this forum.

During the summer and especially during the Edinburgh Festival thousands of people will pass by our frontage. The possibilities for outreach are endless. During this year's Festival a modest 'Friendly presence' has been designed for us by Mary Evans, a Friend from Exeter Meeting who runs Cygnet Youth Training Theatre. We plan to have a lunchtime cabaret, a vegetarian café along with an exhibition of the Quaker Tapestry in the week after Yearly Meeting. If this goes well the Meeting House could become an important Quaker venue in the Edinburgh International Festival, testifying to the vigour and breadth of the Society in Britain today.

Edinburgh is an academic and institutional centre as well as a major tourist city. For this reason Friends operate a Bed and Breakfast scheme, and we hope to extend a warm welcome to many visitors each year.

Ian Ramsey

Watch the spaces
over the rooftops
    laced by birds
    and draped with cloud
    moving 'a tempi'
    from chimney to wall
See between the arches'
stiff and chill perfection
    how windows grace the panoply
    while we are dense receivers
    and makers of half-lives
Then go
as lightly as possible
    clothed in air
    and shod with clay:
    Note the unveiling sun
    indicates East and West

Rhoda R. MacKenzie

YOUNG FRIENDS IN SCOTLAND

Steadily, piece by piece the strands of a diverse and far-flung family are drawn together; a community patiently gathered by a few young Friends from various locations and vocations after two years of gentle persuasion. Scottish Young Friends gatherings have released a resurgence of energy, and friendships are growing. These gatherings meet a need to bring the Society alive for the younger generations, extending the experience of Meeting to an experience of community.

The inspiration behind all this activity has come, in part, from the need for a Scottish Young Friends' gathering outwith the predominantly English based Young Friends' Central Committee. This need was highlighted by the number of Scottish based Young Friends who attended a YFCC weekend held in Glasgow in May 1987. Because Young Quakers in Scotland are isolated from Quaker activity by distance they appreciated the involvement with a wider range of Friends. The new Scottish base now draws in Young Friends from all over Scotland.

This is not to say that travel problems have been solved, as Scottish Young Friends are still up to five hours apart and financial resources compound these geographical barriers. An exuberant and hardy sixteen braved a New Year ferry crossing over to Arran at Hogmanay; but Aberdeen, Glasgow and Edinburgh are the usual centres for activity every three months or so.

Students, married couples, musicians, 9-5ers and all other sorts make up our diverse group.

Everyone adds in their own way to the gatherings which are sometimes theme or activity oriented or simply sociable. We tend to use our own resources to develop a theme. We recently organised for ourselves a weekend on "Imaging a World Without Weapons". Northern Friends Peace Board and others have also helped us.

There are no business meetings so far and we have yet to decide what direction we should be taking as regards group witness on social issues - for instance the Poll Tax. Gradually, through socialising, discussing issues and playing games, our knowledge of each other has developed and we are more aware of each others' far flung needs. Friendships are growing which hold the group together.

Any revolutions coming from this small circle are yet to be fully realised.

Piers Voysey

We gather quietly in the darkened room,
Soft music soothes away
The tension of the day,
We are at peace.

Silence - only the glowing flame of the candle.
Response - from the quiet place in my soul.

Silence -   only the breathing life-force
               As we and mankind are healed.
Silence -   only the clasping of hands
               together
               As we send peace to the world.

Beatrice A. Watson

This Music Stand in iron and brass was designed and made by John Creed of Glasgow Meeting, a silversmith, whose work includes items for domestic use, civic and other ecclesiastic pieces for the churches in Scotland. The work has recently diversified into wrought ironwork.

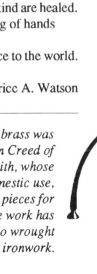

An Orkney Wedding

This is an account of the Marriage of Julian Bradley and Elizabeth Charters at the home of Sandy and William McEwen, North Flaws, South Ronaldsay; the first Quaker wedding in Orkney.

"When we had removed the old car, the bits of engine, swept the floor and white-washed the walls, we began to believe we could be married in the barn at North Flaws. Flowers arrived from everywhere, wild flowers from the Moss, ragged robin, meadowsweet and wild irises, bunches of helse, roses, hanging baskets and pots of geraniums. But at the end of two days of preparation, Saturday evening was wet and we discovered that the usual Sunday morning ferry from John o'Groats would not be running as the rudder needed maintenance. Several friends were relying on this ferry so we asked a local fisherman, but he was doubtful about tides and the wind, even if we could contact these various friends.

On the Sunday morning of 10th July we woke to rain beating on the windows but as people arrived the skies cleared and the boatman decided it was safe to cross.

Eventually at 12.00 in glorious sunshine our last guest arrived, sea-soaked but happy.

So the Meeting gathered as we marvelled at the fullness with which our prayers had been answered. There were about fifty of us, including Ernle Beyts, the registering officer from Aberdeen. The shafts of sunlight fell across the silent Meeting. After we had made our promises, we exchanged tokens of our love, an Orcadian ring and a wooden plaque on which there is painted a rose, and the words 'friendship, love, joy and kindness'. The blessed and carefully chosen words of friends

were interspersed with the calls of the curlew, oyster catcher and common gull adding their blessing from the rooftop.

Even though we met, talked, laughed, ate, danced and listened to bagpipes in the barn until late that night, the special quality of the Meeting remained and was noticeable a week later. Friends brought coloured wool for us to weave into a God's Eye on two branches of rosewood, the only wood we could find on South Ronaldsay!

It was truly the perfect wedding for us, and although we planned much of it, there was so much that could not have been planned and which we could never have dreamed of. We are sure this is as much due to the thoughts and prayers of those who were not present physically as those who were.

Dundee Meeting House

A 114-year old sign astonished builders and architects in Dundee, when it was unexpectedly uncovered above a city centre shop undergoing alterations beneath the Meeting House on the second floor.

The stone lettered 'Meeting House' sign was found under a metal sheet. Friends have an original drawing of what it looked like in 1873, but presumed that the words 'Meeting House' were merely painted on. If it could be, it is hoped that the sign can be incorporated into the new design.

Children's Views...

OSStN

puts litter in its propr place

No snok

NO smokeing

No fighting

Pease

pease

animals free

Ossian Butler (Aged 9)

Dear Grown-ups of today,

As a child I am quite concerned about the future. Please can you look after the world so it is in reasonable condition for when we are in charge of it. For egsample, we would like the ozone layer to last for at least a few more generations. We want a CLEAN world so DON'T DROP LITTER. Please cooperate with each other and leave the world in good condition for us.

Yours Sincerly,

Rachel Bryers and todays children.

Look after the future, PLEASE. ozone FRIENDLY

HAIR SPRAY

Rachel Bryers (Aged 10)

Some Scottish Friends

Our Meetings encompass many types and many conditions. The pieces which follow seek to portray a small cross-section of Scottish Friends, including two whose recent deaths have saddened us, two from backgrounds not frequently represented amongst us and one younger Friend whose experience of growing up in a Quaker environment has meant much to her.

Nicola Maharg invited Ian and Alex to share their experiences with Friends. *Ian Richardson is thirty two and a member of West of Scotland Monthly Meeting. He lives in Glasgow.*

What attracted you to The Society of Friends?

I worked a lot with the peace movement. I used to pass Glasgow Meeting House and met a Quaker through Centre Peace. I decided to drop in on a Sunday meeting. I gradually got into it. I like the ministries although I find ministering hard because I am conscious of being hard of hearing so I tend to shout. Because I am hard of hearing I value hearing one ministry at a time. I think the silence brings you closer to God. Everyone has got something to say so it's worth listening in the first place. In meeting I say something to them and they say something to me. My friend Mohammed from round the corner says, 'How do you know Friends are praying and not

thinking about putting the kettle on?' I say, 'Well generally they are praying.'

Has your lifestyle changed since you joined Friends three years ago?

I live more simply. My flat is basic. I have two sets of clothes because it's all I need. I dress simply. Society pushes on you a set of beliefs through advertising. It's a waste of resources.

I think more about ecology now. When I take action I don't pay my fines but go to jail and send the money to charities like 'Save the Children Fund'. That way it will be spent better. My attitudes have changed since I joined Friends. I listen more to what people are saying.

I know you have taken some direct action as a result of your beliefs. Could you tell me a bit more about that?

I have been in prison about eight times in the last two years for peace and animal rights action. I was done for cutting the fence at

27

Upper Heyford. I've been nabbed for taking action at Faslane. I was arrested for sitting in front of the cattle trucks at Duke Street slaughter house in Glasgow. Tolstoy summed it up, 'Where you have slaughter houses you have wars'.

How does that action tie in with your Quaker beliefs?

The way I see it, a Christian cannot go to war. If you go to war you have to have an enemy and that enemy is a human just like you or I. How can you kill a human being? There's other methods we could use without damage. If we take Jesus words 'love your enemy' how can we kill? War has never solved problems.

How do you feel about your own meeting here in Glasgow?

I think you can feel the same as a Quaker anywhere. I think if we look at the differences and where people live we could go on and on about that. We should look at what unites us not what's different. I go to Wednesday meeting. It's a time to meet although it would be nice if we had some new faces. We don't get to know each other enough on Sundays and Wednesdays. We come and go and that's it. I enjoyed 'Gifts and Discoveries' - getting to meet and discuss and build up a better picture of religious and Quaker life. If I know people then I can speak. If I don't know people I am wary because I don't know what they are thinking if I shout too much.

There's an air in our meeting house that makes you feel comfortable. I didn't get much support for animal rights, but it's o.k. We all go for different things - it's just where they come on our list.

And the future?

I'm going on the European Peace Pilgrimage in 1992. We're walking 2,600 miles in seven months across America from peace camp to peace camp. That's the time they say Trident will come over here.

Alex McGinty is 57 and a member of West of Scotland Monthly Meeting. He is 'married, with two adults' and goes to Glasgow Meeting.

What led you to apply for membership?

I'd been coming for eight years. I hadn't been anywhere as long. I had been a spiritual tramp - you name it I was in it. Quakers seemed more caring for the individual. I felt within myself that I wasn't part of the Meeting unless I joined. So I wrote a letter. I didn't tell anyone. I had been sitting on the fence and could get off and get out or get off and get in. So I got in.

Why did you delay applying for so long?

I felt I might not be accepted because of being working class, and my accent. I'm not well educated, but I knew it's where I wanted to belong.

What attracted you to the Society of Friends?

Here you can express your own feelings and how you think . Here everyone can have their say - it's a great thing. I like the spiritual atmosphere of the Meeting where I can think for myself and find my own version of God there, and other people's too.

It's changed me a lot. I used to be quite a violent person at times - a bit of a tear away. I would just steam in - it's either me or you Jimmy. Now I've turned away from all of that and back off.

Quakers help me keep together. Unemployment - it's a big shock. I'm trying to accept it and live on what I get. It's just an existence after 43 years of work. A feeling that nobody cares. I do wee odd jobs for the meeting house. I've been to Glenthorne and Abernethy family gathering. I love being with so many Quakers.

What meetings do you go to?

Wednesday nights because every weekend I go hillwalking and cycling. There were four of us here this evening. I go to Monthly Meetings and try not to miss any. It's very interesting and it's good to have your say. Strong feelings are not enough - people should attend Monthly Meeting when they have the chance. I appreciate the honesty at our business meetings - that didn't happen in some of my jobs.

You went to Woodbrooke too. Can you tell me about it?

Magic, pure magic. It was an unemployment weekend with people in the same position. We were with the professionals who knew the system. I saw a number of people who were professional and unemployed. We had discussions talking about what we did from when we left school to coming to Woodbrooke.

I had started as a message boy. My last job was Assistant Gardener for the Parks Department. I was eight years teaching boys gardening and then the scheme stopped - no more money. There was no redundancy money. Then I applied for a job looking after the plants. They told me I was too old at 57. For any job I'm too old.

So at Woodbrooke they gave me something and I gave to them. It was good to be with people who had a share of it.

What do you spend your time doing?

I've been mountaineering for twenty years. I've been cycling since I was fourteen and now I've gone back to it. I do Munroes but that's not my aim - to notch them up. I'm happy to just be in the mountains and country-side. If I did Munores I did them and if not I didn't. I do it in lousy weather and in good.

I've learned a bit about their history. Duncan Ban McIntyre was a Gaelic poet who wrote pibroch music. He was illiterate - could neither read nor write. He wrote a poem in praise of Ben Doran at Oich Glen, three miles up the road to Bridge of Orchy. It was all taken down by the minister - five hundred verses in praise of a mountain. I went to Rhum with Dan Watson, an old Friend, five years in a row and dossed out in the bothy there.

The camera's a hobby and the binoculars for the birds. I always carry a book of flora and fauna and the book of poetry of John Betjeman. My favourite is the first one about the old woman, 'Death in Leamington'

Where you come from?

I'm Glasgow born and bred. I was brought up in Kinning Park in a room and kitchen in the garret until the building was falling down. Then we moved to a new house with a bathroom, our own green*(garden)*, a bedroom and an inside toilet. That was posh - like a palace. For the washing we had to go down to the steamy at seven in the morning to get a place.

My Dad's side, like many Glasgow families, came originally from Ireland. They came via Islay where my great grandparents lived at Port Charlotte. They came to Glasgow in the late 1800's for the work - shipbuilding on the Clyde. My Dad became unemployed. It broke his heart when he had to join the army. He said he wanted to earn money but not by killing people. He was away six years.

My daughter stays with us and my son's moved out this week. They're getting rid of five hundred workers where he is and we don't know yet if he stays. My wife Irene - she makes the soup for Wednesday meetings.

Kenneth and Kathleen Laurie have played an active part in the life of Friends in Scotland over very many years. Kathleen Laurie died in November 1988.

Quiet times

I grew up with a love of, and access to, beautiful country, and was able to spend long periods sitting still on a hillside, or in a wood, until I felt part of it, and joined to the rhythm of the Universe. At 15 years old, in the dormitory, when the younger boarders were asleep, I was able to look out to the distant Welsh Hills and to listen to the owls. Here I said my prayers, and again 'got in touch'. This way of 'Quiet Times' has never left me, but alone it is not enough.

The World is full of mysteries, and it is difficult to be sure that the Creative Spirit of the Universe is a God of Love. As Christians we believe that, in Jesus of Nazareth we have a revelation of this Spirit, and an affirmation that we can have a close relationship with this Spirit. This will express itself by making our lives channels through which God can show love to all creatures, including our fellow men. This relationship does not come easily to most of us, it is a way of life which needs discipline. No-one who wishes to have a

31

healthy body neglects to set certain times aside to give it food, sleep etc. We cannot make or keep friends unless we have time to spend with them, yet we neglect to leave time to feed our souls, and to cultivate this friendship with God that Jesus says we could have.

My main time for this is early morning. I get up at 6am, make a pot of tea, then go back to bed 'sitting comfortably' for half an hour. This time I spend in reading, in prayer, in asking God's Blessing on the Day, especially on each person for whom I have a special concern and also in trying to be quiet and listen (I'm not good at that), in saying thank you and in asking help to face the day. Then I take cups of tea to the family and each one can get a quiet spell and not begin the day in a rush.

All day long I can then do what Brother Lawrence, Thomas Kelly and many others suggest - just talk to God as if He were in the kitchen or shop or wherever I am, and so try to keep a very matter of fact consciousness of His Presence.

When the children were young morning quiet turned into a morning serial invented by Dad and life had to be adapted to their wants. I think that each person should find out which is the best way for them to get quiet and try to discipline themselves to keep some time each day for it. The habit grows, and in these days of rush, strain and noise, becomes increasingly valuable.

I have been talking of individual 'Quiet Times' but our religion is one of 'Community' and is not complete unless we join together for praise, thanksgiving, prayer and listening; this is where our Meeting for Worship has its place. Friends who live far from a settled 'Meeting' could join with other worshipping communities and remember that "where two or three are gathered together there am I in the midst".

A Man of Integrity

John was born in 1915, in a small mining village, Gorebridge, about ten miles from Edinburgh. He was second in a family of six, one baby died in infancy, the family was very close knit and right up to hit death, he kept in touch. In financial matters, his family always asked his advice, given willingly, and always taken. Leaving school at 15 years, through study and exams he reached executive grade in the Post Office, having started as a boy messenger.

He spent 6 years in the Army during WW2, and was for some time in India, a country which fascinated him, and it may be, that this was where his thoughts turned to things spiritual. His greatest memory was of seeing the Himalayas and climbing in the foothills.

After the war he married Nancy and they had two children, Jean and Graeme. Nancy started attending Stafford Street Meeting when the children were small, and some time later he started attending, eventually joining.

His wide knowledge of finance was an asset to the Society of Friends in Scotland, and he served faithfully for many years as Treasurer to S. E. Scotland Monthly Meeting and General Meeting.

John was not an outgoing man in the strict sense of the word - his loves were his family, climbing and walking, and music. He was not a party goer, but liked to see others enjoy life in their own way. He was only ever truly himself in the Scottish mountains which he knew like the back of his hand. There he could commune with himself and his God in an atmosphere of complete silence. He was heard to say that among the mountains he was "cut down to size." Eighteen years before his death he suffered a severe heart attack, and his family had to face the fact that he would climb again, a difficult decision for them. But he did climb for another 17 years and not long before his death he had a climbing holiday in his beloved West Highlands. He also enjoyed fell walking, and along with Nancy, enjoyed several holidays at the Quaker Guest House Glenthorne, in Grasmere.

A memorial service was held in August in St. Mark's Unitarian Church and Friends from all over Scotland came to pay their respects and show their love for John. He always said he wanted no fuss after his death, and his funeral was a quiet family affair. But it would not have been right to deny Friends the opportunity to say goodbye.

His favourite Biblical text was from the Book of Genesis: "And behold, I am with thee, and will keep thee in all places where thou goest."

Margaret Woolgrove is 18 and is studying at St. Andrews University

Journeyings...

I was recently asked about what I thought the future of the Society of Friends was; where it was going, and what was happening to its young people. My questioner said she had seen a substantial drop in the number of child attenders, and that whilst she, in her youth, had attended the whole hour of Meeting from eight years up, the young people of today's meetings have their children and young persons' classes, with only a brief interval in the actual Meeting for Worship, right up until their teens, at which time their numbers start to dwindle and their faces become less and less familiar in the weekly ranks.

I could only answer this Friend's query from my own particular experience, which, as with all experience is unique and individual.

For the first ten years of my life I lived with my family in Cornwall, and we regularly (though somewhat grudgingly at times on my part!) attended one of the 3 local Meetings. In my tenth year, we pulled up our roots and headed

North, to a spot near Oban, on the west coast of Scotland. Our nearest Meeting on the map was held on Mull, a nearby island, but it was both a geographic and economic impossibility for us to meet with Friends there. In our first year especially, we made fairly regular trips across to Dunblane Meeting - a 180 mile round trip. A year or two later, the 'unofficial' family meeting for worship held in our home became an 'official entity', and meetings on the first Sunday of the month became a regular feature of our lives, with our ranks often swelling to an unprecedented size, what with local attenders and visiting Friends. Indeed, I believe I would attribute much of my spiritual questing to the influence visiting Friends had on me. Friends from Australia, the United States of America, Holland, Norway and from all round Britain often came to Meeting, and if not staying with us for longer, at least stayed for lunch. I learnt a lot from just listening to the 'grown ups' talk about the Society and its work. We met some truly wonderful people in this way - people who demonstrated to me the beauty and true purpose of life as expressed in Quakerism at its best. I owe a lot to them all. Without these people, and the support of my family, I wonder whether the message of Quakerism would have yet reached me...

I valued the 'rural' experience of my childhood Quakerism very much - it was not unknown for the family to 'meet' on the lawn outside, or on the rocks of a nearby bay, in the wondrous simplicity of the natural world.

So, where is the Society going? Well, I strongly believe that the attitudes inculcated into the young people of today through the example and lifestyle of their parents is crucial. Unless young people recognise some quality in their home life which they would wish to imitate in their own lives, the Quaker experience will be lost. It is not something which can be taught, it is a 'something' which is part of an inbuilt, subconscious learning process. Perhaps it is a question of ensuring that the 'light within' is not being hidden, but rather is free to shine forth over all the world.

For me, the importance of my Quaker heritage was not the treks over to Dunblane for a 'proper' Meeting for Worship, but rather the meeting of many 'fellow travellers' on their spiritual journeys as they passed through Scotland. The evidence of God all around me, in the rugged beauty of the hills and coastline of the west coast of Scotland, and God in the home and the hearts of family and friends meant a great deal.

Truly is it stated by George Fox that "Love of God is the ground of all true love".

The Rugged Road

Life is full of its ups and downs
As so many know so well.
And we might wonder why we've to battle along
With so little success for to tell.

Sometimes we're high, but so often so low,
And we wonder what might happen next,
And if things don't work out as we think they should
We then might say "now I'm real vexed".

But the important thing it seems to me
In this life with its ups and downs
Is the way we react as we battle along
Is it positive, negative, smiles or frowns.

And the best way it seems is to be well prepared
And be positive what e'er come along.
And then we may find after passing each test
That we travel along with a song.

Fred Jones

POEMS by EDNA BEYTS

Written in 1981 when she had begun to realise she was suffering from Alzheimer's Disease.

Sunday Nov 29th

Purple the hills
In the evening light,
Golden the bracken
In the late sun.
No movement
apparent
Save for the traveller
Crossing this lonely
place.

Once there were
people
living here,
Tumbled stones,
An odd corner
Still standing
Remain
But the people
Vanished
Long ago,
Forced from their
precarious
Living - out

Across the seas
Where they settled
Prospered
And multiplied.

Now here
All is silence-
For a short time
The guns of
Sportsmen
Shatter the
Silence.

They do not see
The shades
Or hear the cry of
Lamentation
Why should they
There is nobody
Here

Walking Back to Quaker History

Dear Lord I'm growing older
and I feel I've lost the way.
My confidence is shattered
Morale at lowest ebb.
Perhaps I've been too arrogant
I was busy and allowed myself
no time to contemplate.
Now I've time in plenty
But I cannot concentrate.
My errant thoughts
Distract me -
Then I smell the burning stew -
With all those good "Advices"
(I've read them through and through)
But I still cannot manage
To do as I would do.
There are some
I greatly envy
(Forgive that sin as well)
who without complaint
or fuss -
Just grow old graciously.

Edna Beyts

37

A Bygone World

Deserted croft, Gartymore, Sutherland.

Cross the A9 from my cottage, walk up the Brae and onto Gartymore and you enter a bygone world which is still a way of life in much of Sutherland and Caithness. It is a wilderness of heather and bracken, criss-crossed by old peat roads where you can walk alone for miles with only sheep, buzzards and harriers for company. The air is like wine and for miles you can look back onto the sea. This is the land of the Highland Clearances. I have been shown photographs of grandparents who were evicted from tiny crofts in the Strath of Kildonan to make way for the sheep of the rich landowners. The bitterness has not yet gone, but there's a welcome too, and on my rambles I've been invited into remote homes for cups of tea and a "blether" by lovely people. I don't know them, but they know me, a stranger, and where I have come to live.

Marlène Walker - Colward

*Dove Ring designed
for a Peace Card by
Julian Leoidsson of
Orkney Meeting*

A QUAKER WITNESS FOR PEACE

A Statement by Helen Steven in Dumbarton Sheriff Court in Defence of Action taken at Faslane on the 4th April 1984

I do not wish to deny that on April 4th, the anniversary of the death of Martin Luther King, I was inside the Faslane Submarine Base, and that I was there as a deliberate act. However I pled 'not guilty' to the charges because had I done otherwise I would have been guilty of far greater crimes against my conscience and against humanity.

If I may, I would like to outline very briefly the reasons for so acting, not so much as mitigation of guilt, but rather as a declaration of intent, for as long as these bases remain, I must continue to act as my conscience guides.

My charge is that I entered a protected area without authority or permission. My claim is that I had authority – the authority of my Christian conviction that a gospel of love cannot be defended by the threatened annihilation of millions of innocent people. It can never be morally right to use these ghastly weapons at any time, whether first, or as unthinkable retaliation after we ourselves are doomed.

I acted also with the authority of the nameless millions dying of starvation now because we choose to spend £11.5 billions on Trident whilst a child dies every 15 seconds.

I am further authorised by my 13 year-old Vietnamese god-daughter whose guardian I am. She was adopted and brought to Scotland to take her away from the unspeakable horror of the Vietnam war. If all that I have done is to bring her closer to the nuclear holocaust, I stand convicted by her of the most cynical inhumanity.

I am charged under an Act giving control and disposal of land to the Queen, the Lords Spiritual and Temporal, the Commons assembled in Parliament and eventually the Secretary of State. I believe the world is God's creation. This beautiful, delicate world in all its infinite wonder is threatened with extinction. That to me is blasphemy.

Dove Ring designed

And so, out of love, love of my god-daughter, love of my world, I had to act. If I see that base at Faslane as morally wrong and against my

Non - violence on the Inside

deepest convictions - as wrong as the gas chambers of Belsen and Dachau, as wrong as the deliberate starvation of children - then by keeping silent I condone what goes on there.

On April 4th, I made a choice. I chose to create the dream of another way. My only crime is not working hard enough, or long enough, or soon enough towards the fulfilment of the dream. If my actions were a crime, then I am guilty.

Helen was found guilty and was fined £30. She refused to pay and was then sentenced to seven days imprisonment.

Helen Steven wrote about her experiences during a 7 day prison sentence spent in Cornton Vale Women's Prison, Stirling, in The Friend of 26 April, 1985. She spoke of the challenge she faced in prison to communicate with 'the opposition' - the sheriff, police and prison officers - and with other prisoners.

"Undoubtedly the aspect which troubled me most was the readiness to be oppressed of so many of the women inside, and their deprivation. One woman shivered with cold all night because she didn't think she was allowed to turn on the heater; another had never touched a real carnation in her life; one woman with a four-year sentence was allowed to see her 18-month-old child once a month. What was needed was help in taking control of their own lives, and yet prison was removing every capacity for decision-making. Even TV was compulsory with no choice of programme.

Repression was being steadily reinforced in a constant daily round, the more insidious for being apparently benevolent.

"The night that I went to prison, the fence went up at Molesworth. Reflecting on the news on my own in my cell, I reached my lowest point of futility and helplessness against the seemingly inevitable juggernaut of military might. Expect change, live hope, don't let the dream die. Now more than ever, I am convinced that change happens through the gentle persistent meeting of person to person quietly reaching out to that of God."

Arms Around Scotland

On the 5th October 1986, 48 000 ordinary people from all over Scotland linked hands to put their 'Arms Around Scotland'. Many Friends, including children, took part. Here are two accounts of the event by members of Glasgow Meeting Sunday School

We put our arms around Scotland on the 5th October. All over Scotland, ordinary people turned out to demonstrate for peace. Young children, teenagers, ladies and men and old people all went to stand at certain points around Scotland to hold hands from Glasgow to Grangemouth to put their arms around Scotland.

We saw banners and four helicopters and on Voyager (the T.V. programme) it showed pictures from the line. We were there to show to other people that we don't want nuclear war in Scotland. We all hope that we shall send the message across to people who want bombs that not many people want bombs or other weapons in Scotland.

All along the line everybody was happy because lots of people had joined in and they were glad of other people's company.

Ruth Baldry (Glasgow Meeting) age 10

I was standing by the road with Rachel after 3 o'clock. We had been holding hands and holding up our banners. Suddenly we saw a skeleton coming. It was a tall man dressed up in a white mask and wore a big black coat with a big black hood. He was a very frightening skeleton. He was trying to tell us not to throw bombs because they turn people to skeletons.

Claire Crawford (Glasgow Meeting) Age 8

Let us now praise...

We have our own "Familiar Friend" in Scotland. Bill Aitken, of Dunblane Meeting, was editor of Scottish Friends Newsletter for many years. "Let us now praise" is one of his editorials, from the June 1985 issue. We also print later in this book a second of his editorials, "A Poet's Question" (February 1985)

Lewis Fry Richardson, a birthright Quaker and a distinguished scientist, was principal of Paisley Technical College from 1929 to 1940, and during that period and after, he and his wife played an active role in Glasgow Meeting. His distinction as a meteorologist was recognized in 1972 when an extension to the Met Office HQ, opened by the Prime Minister, was named the Richardson Wing. But his keen mind had many interests beyond meteorology. He had been a conscientious objector in WW1, serving with the F A U in France and he applied his "rare mathematical talent" to a consideration of the causes of wars and how to maintain peace. Richardson's "daring attempt to deal mathematically with foreign politics" and his statistical analysis of the arms race make him a pioneer in peace studies, and it is entirely appropriate that his name is perpetuated in the Richardson Institute for Conflict and Peace Research at Lancaster University.

When Betsy and I moved to the west of Scotland in 1958, Richardson had been dead for more than five years, but our first home there was in a house that belonged to his son Olaf (named after the author Olaf Stapledon, whom Richardson had met while working with the FAU); we came to respect and admire him and from him we learned something of his father. This contact prompted our interest in the biography just published by Oliver M. Ashford, *Prophet or Professor? The Life and Work of Lewis Fry Richardson* (Bristol: Adam Hilger). It is a book to be read and pondered: full of interest, packed with memorably quotable anecdotes, exhilarating and exciting. His life-long devotion to the cause of peace is inspiring. The "Life" concludes with the minute of the Friends memorial service in Glasgow, but the "Work" continues and develops.

The minute reads: " Tributes were paid to the life and character of Lewis Richardson. Mention was made of the integrity of his professional life, of the sacrifices he had often made for the sake of his sense of truth and righteousness. Along with his outstanding intellectual gifts went courage and gaiety, and he was filled with a deep desire that we should live and work so that future generations might enjoy a better world than that ...(of) today."

43

PEACE
cannot be kept
by force
It can only be
achieved by
understanding

EINSTEIN

Quaker Peace Cards began in 1980, when an Edinburgh Friend brought to her Preparative Meeting her concern to contribute to peace work by publishing cards carrying a peace message.

Since then several cards have been published and sold worldwide, including one designed by a group of children in Edinburgh Meeting. In 1986 a Peace Prints competition was held in conjunction with Edinburgh Printmakers Workshop and the winning design became the new card for that year.

For information, write to Peace Cards, Friends House, 7 Victoria Terrace, Edinburgh EH1 2JL.

Peace House

I suppose the idea of Peace House was originally conceived in Vietnam fifteen years ago, when Ellen Moxley and I were working in orphanages there. Only a pipe dream, a gleam in the eye. "Wouldn't it be wonderful to have a house where people came to study peace." And just about as distant as Saigon from Scotland!

Some five years later when we had both returned, and Ellen and I were living in the depths of Dumfriesshire, the idea resurfaced slightly stronger with rather more flesh on its bones. We wrote up a "Proposal for a Scottish Peace Centre", almost as grandiose as its title, and we sent it around our various friends for their reactions. The response was rapid and all too accurate. "You've no money"; "You've not enough contacts". A wise Friend said "Put it on the shelf, and when the time is right you will know and can bring it down again."

In the meantime we simply got on with the job of working for peace. In 1979 I became the justice and peace worker for the Iona Community and in that capacity began to build up a huge network of contacts, friends and activists, literally all over the world. We moved to a tiny cottage near Dunblane, and sometimes it seemed as if all these many friends had passed through our cottage. Ellen was already running a small peace centre in three rooms. And so it might have continued - with two rather frenzied peace activists - one dashing around the country giving talks and workshops, the other slowly and steadily building up local peace groups and cooking endless meals - had it not been for the trust and generosity of two of our Iona Community friends.

It was while walking in the woods near our home in the spring of 1983 that Graeme and Mary told us that they had such faith in our dream of a peace centre that they would like to give us £10,000 to make it begin to happen. With this confidence spurring us on we took the proposal off the shelf and blew the dust from it. The time was exactly right. The peace movement in the early eighties was at its peak, and needed a focal point of consolidation and inspiration in Scotland. Our work in non-

violence training had given us both much greater experience to enable us to undertake the venture. This was beginning to widen out into broader issues of social justice; we most certainly had the contacts; now we had some money.....nothing could stop us!

Perhaps if we had known some of the hassles which lay ahead in the next three years we might have joined the army! Initially we formed a housing co-operative of several people to enable us to raise loans. Several properties were visited, in varying stages of ruin and dilapidation, our main problem being to find a place big enough for our then grand ideas, cheap enough for our limited budget, but still having a roof and four walls. Our original idea of eleven people living together as a core community fell apart until we were left with the original trio of Ellen, Marian (Ellen's adopted daughter) and myself.

It was then that we discovered The Old Manse at Greenloaning. A solid square built house with five bedrooms, three big public rooms, kitchen with Raeburn, amazing bathroom (come and visit to find out about it!) and half an acre of garden. It seemed ideal, and especially as it is located at the very centre of Scotland. We raised a loan from the Falkland Community Trust and put in an offer. There were endless legal problems, but after a year of agonising uncertainty we moved in during a blizzard on International Women's Day in March 1987.

Peace House can accommodate seven overnight guests, and up to fifteen for day conferences. We organise a programme, with some courses where we provide the input and others where groups come with their own agenda. In the eighteen months since March 1987 we have had 1,082 visitors, which surely says something about the need for such a place in Scotland - or at least about people's curiosity! Visitors have come from as far afield as Vietnam, North India, Iceland, Namibia, Germany, Czechoslovakia; from all over Britain, and also a growing number of local people. Groups such as Northern Friends Peace Board, Scottish Churches Action for World Development, Christian CND, Clergy for Peace, the Iona Community and the Scottish Peace Centre have become regular fixtures on our calendar. Courses over the past year have been very varied ranging from a visit to Faslane Submarine Base, Young Friends weekend, programme planning with the Woodcraft Folk, an Alternative Christmas, various non-violence workshops, and a week of back breaking work with Quaker International Social Projects ('Work Camps'). Our most popular course has been a workshop for women on anger; our funniest a non-violence weekend with Lochaber CND which began with them breaking and entering through the library window. Our future programme includes a focus on S. Africa; "Turning the Tide" a look at political realities in Scotland, and study weeks around Yearly Meeting in August.

Since our opening two years ago the Peace House Trust has been formed and has given money to enable the Trust to buy Peace House, thus relieving us of the debt burden. Peace House Trust is made up jointly of Friends and Iona Community representatives and now manages the project with Ellen and myself employed to run Peace House.

We pray that Peace House may be a focus for peaceful action for change for many years to come. Do come and visit us and see for yourselves.

Helen Steven
Peace House, The Old Manse
Greenloaning, Braco
Dunblane, FK15 0LY

General Meeting for Scotland has played an active part both in Scottish Churches Council and in the Inter-Church Process. This extract from General Meeting minutes of September 1988 reflects our response to the consultative proposals for Scottish Churches Together.

We have moved on to consider what is required of us at this time regarding the progress towards setting up new ecumenical instruments. Meeting for Sufferings has received, at its meeting on 2nd July, a lengthy draft response to the consultative reports of Working Parties set up as a sequel to the Conference at Swanick in 1987. It is seeking a response from General Meeting for Scotland on the particular proposals for a body to be known as "Scottish Churches Together". This response will form a part of Friends comments of the total document. Following completion of consultation, a report will be published on final proposals, and London Yearly Meeting will be required to reach its conclusions on this when it meets in Aberdeen in 1989.

We welcome without hesitation the movement towards greater unity amongst Scottish Churches. Friends have been pleased to play their part as full members of Scottish Churches Council and have valued this tangible partnership with other Christians. We see it as a major step forward in Scotland for the Roman Catholic Church to become a part of this expression of the ecumenical movement. We acknowledge that it may be necessary for there to be a credal basis to "Scottish Churches Together." If this is so, we would not wish to argue against that basis for unity, though we might regret the consequences for ourselves.

Our deliberations have, however, strengthened our conviction that it would be right for us to maintain our commitment to the primacy of personal experience and to unity of the Spirit. We draw to the attention of the Working Parties the bases upon which churches have united in Australia and in the Conference of Churches in Aotearoa, New Zealand, and the form of words proposed for the Council of Churches for Wales. We must await the decisions of the Working Party for Scotland and in due course assess what form of association with "Scottish Churches Together" is possible for Friends in Scotland. Whether this is observer status, associate membership or full membership, we shall hope to play our part, and to maintain our fellowship in the Spirit and in its practical out workings with these churches within the united body, with those not in membership of it, and with members of other faiths.

"Life streams through disciples of every race and clime and condition—-it does not press men into a rigid mould of thought or action; rather it would pour its own joy into every mould of humanity." (Wm Charles Braithwaite *Christian Faith and Practice* § 207)

A further minute, of March 1989 comments upon the subsequent proposals for ACTS - Action of Churches Together for Scotland. It concludes: "With humility and with faith ourselves in the possibilities ahead we are encouraged to respond positively to the welcome embrace that is being offered to us and to respond with warmth and acceptance, in the understanding that while words may divide the spirit unites."

Chalice and ciborium used by Pope John Paul II at Open Air Mass, Bellahouston Park, Glasgow, on 1st June, 1982

This was commissioned by the Archdiocese of Glasgow to commemorate the Pope's visit and for future use within the Diocese. Both pieces are designed and hand made by John Creed of Glasgow Meeting. They are hand wrought in sterling silver with the interior of the bowls bright gold plated. The challice has a knob of polished Iona stone.

FIRST CONGRESS OF EXILED YOUTH

The writers are children of a Chilean Friend from the group of refugees who use rooms in Friends' Meeting House, Glasgow. West Scotland Monthly Meeting has given financial support towards attendance at this Congress.

In July 1988, through "La Victoria, Workshop", we were invited to participate in the first Congress of Exiled Youth which took place between the 13th and 30th August 1988 in Buenos Aires, Santiago and the South of Chile.

What did the Congress Mean to us?

Firstly we shared experiences with youngsters from five continents, speaking Spanish with the accents of their 'step-country' and realising that we all shared a double identity and double cultures.

What topics were debated at the Congress?

We talked of the things that affect youth world-wide, namely: love, religion, drugs, alcohol, politics, freedom, democracy etc. We found great difficulty on the topic of religion. Here are the conclusions from the conference statement:

"We, the youth of Latin America, are known world-wide as revolutionaries - youngsters who from childhood learn to use arms and weapons. We would like to say it is not so, the situation is completely the opposite.

Jesus has arrived in Latin America, not as God, but as an ordinary human being, struggling together with the youth for complete agreement that by giving priority to these three principles, it would benefit not only our nation, but the world. The Youth feel that to achieve this peacefully would be a great triumph. But if we have to fight to achieve this, we will - even to the extent of giving our lives. Even though we all love the beauty of life, we do not fear death, because death is our liberation towards the liberation of others.

From the Congress, our Christmas message to humanity is a simple one. Peace and love to the children and social justice to all, so that maybe one day we will live as brothers and sisters."

Finally we would like to give our appreciation and thanks to all the Quaker Friends who helped not only to make this a reality for us, but also for the people of Chile. Il Paz, Amor y Justica Para el '89. *[With peace, love and justice for 1989]*

Angela Paz and Americo Al Hucema

50

Prisoners of Conscience

Each Christmas, many Friends send greetings cards to prisoners of conscience, using addresses provided by Quaker Peace and Service. Jeny Faulkner, of Glasgow Meeting, was delighted to receive a reply this year from a prisoner in Turkey, thanking Friends for their postcards.

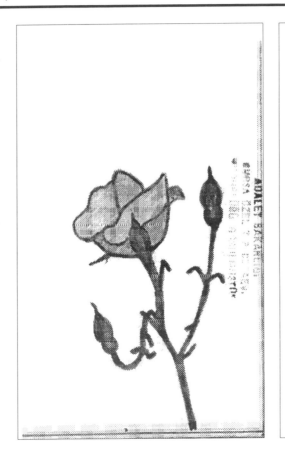

DEAR JENIFER FAULKNER

I received postcards from thirty members of Quaker. Of course I pleased very much.

But should tell that I have no possiblity to answer the all. So I'm sorry. Thankes all of you.

Happy New Year to the all Quakers members.

LOWING GREETINGS.

Keleş KARACA.

A POET'S QUESTION

Another contribution from the pen of Bill Aitken of Dunblane when he was Editor of the Scottish Newsletter.

There is an early poem of Hugh MacDiarmid's, after the German of Rainer Maria Rilke, that commands attention by its very title. It asks the question, 'What Will God Do?', and the reader is compelled to read on to discover what the situation is that the poet imagines God must face. The first line immediately reveals the predicament: 'What would God do if I should die?'

At first one may feel rather startled by the almost blasphemous arrogance of the question. Who does the poet think he is? We recall the psalmist's cry and find its tone more acceptable: 'What is man that thou shouldst remember him, mortal man that thou shouldst care for him?'

But the poet persists in his questioning:

> I am his jar (if I should break?)
> His fountain (if I should run dry?)...
>
> I am the sandals he must wear...

And as we read we are once more forcefully and convincingly reminded of the undeniable truth that even with God in his heaven, all will be right with the world only through human agency. 'God can no more do without us than we can do without him' (Meister Eckhart).

There is a not entirely apocryphal story of the minister who found the beadle working in a much neglected corner of the manse garden and rather sanctimoniously said, 'I always think you are helping God when you work in a garden.' To this the gardener replied with some asperity, 'Weel, minister, ye should hae seen the gairden when God had it a' to dae himsel'.'

The wonders God performs are done by human hands. What will God do if I do not?

Toybox

Had the Princess Royal visited Barlinnie Prison, Glasgow, a week earlier than planned, she might have witnessed the incongruous sight of two burly prison officers carrying a large brightly painted toybox - decorated with birds, bees, flowers and bunnies - into the gaol. The piece which follows describes how "ra wummen wurra toays" arrived in Barlinnie.

Toybox is an independent, voluntary group which seeks to provide play facilities for children visiting family members in Scottish prisons. Being able to play during visits or in the waiting room substantially reduces children's anxiety in the prison setting. Where the children are happy, the adults too are more relaxed and communication improves all round, thus increasing the chances of a good visit and, indirectly, enhancing family relationships.

The idea of play at visits is not new. The first scheme was set up in 1976 at Saughton prison, Edinburgh by Moira MacLean, a Friend and voluntary prison visitor. The Saughton scheme is still going strong, currently trying to increase the number of days on which play facilities are available.

The first Barlinnie group folded in 1984 but was re-established in 1988 with a grant from The Centre for Under Fives (which also funds the play project in Glasgow Sheriff Court) and the enthusiastic support of the Governor, Mr. Alan Walker.

Toybox volunteers, working in pairs, now provide toys in the waiting room at Barlinnie on Tuesday and Thursday afternoons for children visiting relatives on remand. The service has been well received by families and staff alike and since August we have catered for more than 1050 children. The play and toys provide a focus of interest and conversation for the adults as well, all of which helps to reduce stress and pass the time. The work is hectic but fun as most of the children are under school age.

In November 1988 Toybox won the Carnegie Award for voluntary work in the community which we hope will enable us to stimulate the provision of similar facilities in many more Scottish prisons. Lowmoss at Bishopbriggs and Corntonvale have already expressed interest in establishing their own 'Toyboxes'. On the longer term we hope to explore other means of strengthening prisoners' family ties and meeting their needs.

We very much appreciate the help and support of Friends and welcome:

 gifts of small toys in **good** condition, magazines and comics

 donations - even quite small sums of money can top up the Toybox contents. When children play, things get damaged, lost or worn out - often the best loved ones most quickly.

 volunteers who enjoy playing with small children and can spare an afternoon a month on a long term basis (1 year). Our volunteers have to be women - prisoners are extremely sensitive about other men being involved with their wives or partners in any capacity and we have to respect this.

If you can help or would like to know more about Toybox please contact:

Sarah Brown
118 Essex Drive
Glasgow G14 9PD
Tel: 041 959 2914

Prayer from Wormwood Scrubs

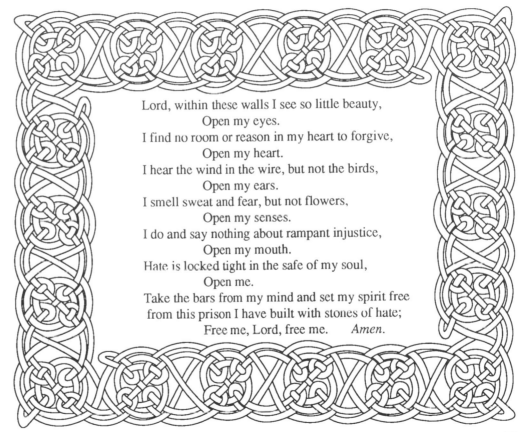

Towards the end of her report on penal affairs to General Meeting in Glasgow in September 1984 Moira MacLean shared with us a moving poem written by a prisoner in Wormwood Scrubs. It is printed now, with acknowledgements to the author and the prison chaplain.

Lord, within these walls I see so little beauty,
　　　Open my eyes.
I find no room or reason in my heart to forgive,
　　　Open my heart.
I hear the wind in the wire, but not the birds,
　　　Open my ears.
I smell sweat and fear, but not flowers,
　　　Open my senses.
I do and say nothing about rampant injustice,
　　　Open my mouth.
Hate is locked tight in the safe of my soul,
　　　Open me.
Take the bars from my mind and set my spirit free
from this prison I have built with stones of hate;
　　　Free me, Lord, free me.　　*Amen.*

Che Open Close community, Royston

Hugh Pyper, of Glasgow Meeting writes here about an inner city project of which he is a trustee.

'Royston? Whit dae ye want tae go there for?' So said the taxi driver when I first ventured to this part of Glasgow. It is officially described as a 'multiple-deprived inner city area'; a few streets of grey council houses and tower blocks on one of the many steep little hills in Glasgow. Quite near the city centre, it is ringed by motorways and major roads which make it a virtual island. It is easy to spot as you drive past on the M8. 'BRITS OUT' is painted in ten-foot-high letters on the retaining wall.

It certainly is not the kind of place to which most people would go by choice. Legend has it that prisoners discharged from Barlinnie jail used to plead to be resettled in the Gorbals rather than in Royston. The levels of every index of social deprivation are frighteningly high. Unemployment, single parent families, drug and alcohol abuse, vandalism, and violence are all facts of life for those in the area. Like some thirty per cent of the homes in Glasgow, damp is a constant misery. Black mould grows on the walls and the only solution is to turn the heating full on and open the windows. No-one can afford that kind of fuel

bill. Glasgow's much-vaunted renaissance has not had much effect yet in Royston.

So, why was I venturing into Royston on a dark winter evening? I was going to visit a small ecumenical community which has been set up in one of the tenement 'closes' in the area. Two attenders at Glasgow meeting had been looking round for some hard-to-let property in the city in order to set up a Christian community. The idea was to work with local young people to explore ways of improving the quality of life. After all kinds of dramas, they had settled in Royston and were beginning to put out feelers to the community. The young people were responding by testing the 'unbreakable' windows by bouncing bricks off them.

Since then, the community has had its successes and failures but is still hanging on. In a staunchly Catholic, indeed Republican, area, the support of the local parish priests has been invaluable and heart-warming though the community still maintains contacts with the small Church of Scotland congregation.

Glasgow is very close to Northern Ireland and the tensions can run high between communities. The bulk of Northern Ireland's Protestants have Scottish origins and the bulk of Scotland's Catholics are the descendants of Irish immigrants.

At the moment, the 'weans' come in when the Junior School comes out for chat and games and a group of teenagers turns up most evenings. Some good friendships have grown up, but things are still unpredictable. Visitors need to be prepared to hear some choice expressions and answer some pretty personal questions. There are also some rather harrowing tales which emerge. Still, there is a great deal of energy and good-will around, and as in all such communities there are people of quite extraordinary faith and determination keeping a candle alight.

There are now plans for setting up a community café and for doing work with single mothers. Of course, money is a problem. The main income is provided by the members of the community who do part-time work, but there are hopes that grants may be available soon. Of course, the community is always grateful for any donations. Even more welcome, though, are offers from people to come and stay for a short or long period and experience life in such an area. Anyone who would be interested can contact them at

The Open Close
283 Roystonhill
Glasgow G21

In April 1989, domestic rates in Scotland gave way to the community charge - commonly known as the poll tax. The new tax has been widely criticized and condemned as unfair and inequitable. The complexities of registration and collection continue to plague the local authorities charged with its administration, and a variety of protest action ranging from disruption to determined non payment continues.

What has been the response of Friends in Scotland to this issue? Our Friend, Alastair McIntosh addressed South East Scotland Monthly Meeting on 11 May 1988:

"In my most formative years during the 1960's and 1970's, I saw some poverty, but not degradation and hopelessness, in the crofting community amongst which I was brought up on the Isle of Lewis.... The hopes of the sixties affirmed, in the words of the Woodstock song, that far from some being unwanted and useless, 'we are stardust, we are golden', and this vision seemed to extend itself right across the range of social class and offered real hope of working towards a less caste-ridden society.

"But the 1980's have revealed that the days of greed, undue privilege and exploitation are not over yet in Britain...the community charge, more than any other reform, seems to me to expose a savage trait of the privileged and powerful in looking after their own interests without adequate concern for the weak and powerless."

He continued by contending that the charge is UNJUST, because it takes no account of the extent to which people living in different areas benefit from local amenities, or of their ability to pay - their taxable capacity. A survey carried out by Cheshire County Council revealed that approximately twice as much gets spent on services in the more affluent areas than in the poorest ones. Households earning less than £100 a week will on average see nearly 4% of their income going on the community charge, while for households earning an excess of £500 per week, the figure will be less than 1%.

He contended that the community charge is UNFAIR. Those living below the poverty line will be liable to pay 20% of their poll tax. The government claims that state benefits will be adjusted to compensate for this, but the benefit increases will be 20% of the average level of community charge paid throughout the country, leaving many claimants losing out.

Thirdly, he stated, the community charge is UNDEMOCRATIC. He cited evidence of people disenfranchising themselves by failing to put themselves on the electoral register. Finally he contended that it is ANTISOCIAL. It is a disincentive for groups of adults to live together under one roof, compared to the rates system. This could have an impact on elderly relatives or teenage children. It will also have an effect on the housing market, removing incentives to move from a larger to a smaller house and thus reducing the supply of family-sized homes on the market. Its effect on the property market may also include sharp increases in house prices, making it harder for young families and those less well off to get a foothold.

Alastair McIntosh suggested that Friends should issue a statement of opposition to the community charge and of solidarity with those who will suffer unfairly from its consequences; that they should provide moral support to those who, through poverty or on principle, attempt to frustrate or even refrain from the processes of registration and payment; and that those who will benefit from the introduction of the community charge should consider whether it is right to hold on to this revenue - they might join with others in forming a redistributive fund.

The concern was further considered by General Meeting for Scotland in June 1988, and the minute reads, in part: "We believe that the Community charge raises serious moral issues for Christians, who have a commitment to the achievement of a just social order. We fear that the community charge proposals pose a serious threat to civil liberties."

Friends have written to the Secretary of State for Scotland, and to other politicians, and the replies received have been detailed, but predictable. Some Friends have sought to research the impact of the charge on individuals, families and communities and have lobbied their local M.P.s to some effect. Others have campaigned over details of the poll tax legislation, particularly as it affects those who are mentally handicapped, or those living in some form of sheltered accommodation or institution. An unknown number of Friends have adopted delaying devices, or have determined to take the consequences of non payment, whilst others have passed on their "gains" to charity - if this is done by covenant there is the added bonus of securing the tax benefit.

It is still too early to know what impact the widespread anti-poll tax campaigning in Scotland has had, though it is apparent that the Government has not been forced to change its mind. Another Scottish Friend, Peter Christy, has concluded that:

"Quakers could, with their unique mix of worldly knowledge and prayerful consideration, make a significant contribution to British society by taking up the challenge of working out how to pay for our society, to enable growth and development into a world we would be proud to pass on to our heirs."

AIDS

*EDINBURGH
FRIENDS'
INVOLVEMENT
WITH THE SUBJECT
OF AIDS/HIV*

In mid 1983, HIV (the causative virus of AIDS) entered a cohort of about 2,000 people in Edinburgh who habitually injected themselves intravenously with heroin. From that time on, over half of these people have tested positive for antibody to the virus, and a substantial proportion of those who test negative may well still be infected. There are still thought to be between 2,000 and 3,000 habitual drug abusers in Edinburgh .

The majority of such people are young and come from socially-deprived areas of the city. More than one third are women, and more than 50 children have been born to HIV seropositive women who are either drug abusers or the sexual partners of drug abusers. It is anticipated that over the next decade a substantial proportion of these people will die of AIDS. There are also fears of a spread into the more general heterosexual population.

Friends, encouraged by Frank Boulton, are responding to this challenge. In early 1988, an ecumenical movement (the "Ecumenical AIDS Support Team", or EAST) was started. This aimed to develop spiritual and practical support for anyone affected by HIV infection. In late 1988 an offshoot - "Positive Help" - designed to supply trained volunteers to help in practical tasks began. Friends are represented by Frank Boulton, and it is anticipated that further active involvement of Friends will develop.

Until her untimely death in 1987, Lisa Boulton had a very special concern for the AIDS problem, particularly the difficulties developing in Central Africa where she had lived for many years. She campaigned in Edinburgh to increase awareness of the African dimension of AIDS. The Lisa Boulton Fund was established in her memory to promote help for people infected by HIV. As an initial measure, Friends are helping to organise the supply of protective medical materials to clinics in Central Africa where HIV infection is rife, using visitors to those countries as couriers, and also through the help of other charitable agencies.

61

the early period in aberdeen

We know that Meetings were held in Scotland from 1653, and visits from English Friends began soon after. This is an extract from papers on the history of Quakers in the Aberdeen area prepared by DELIA SEAGER.

Quakerism spread in Scotland fairly rapidly, and in 1657 George Fox spent several months visiting Glasgow, Edinburgh, Perth, Fife and the Highlands - finding the latter not very welcoming! The first English Quaker to visit Aberdeen appears to have been John Burnyeat from Cumberland in 1658, but there seems to have been little obvious growth in the Society here until William Dewsbury visited in 1662.

Several people are recorded as having become "convinced" then, including Alexander Jaffray (chief magistrate), Margaret Molleson and Margaret Scott (both wives of magistrates), and Elizabeth Goodall (wife of a merchant). The interest of these names is that they were clearly people of standing in the community. Indeed, Alexander Jaffray had been Provost of Aberdeen two or three times. Many more people were convinced soon after, and the public preachers began to get alarmed "that so many both of the higher and lower classes withdrew from their communion". Persecution followed for about the next twenty years, the leaders of it being Bishop Scougal of Aberdeen and Archbishop Sharpe, who

was described as "an unprincipled man". Numerous Friends were imprisoned in the Tolbooth in Aberdeen, and had the audacity to preach from the windows to the populace below - until the windows were stopped up! Massive fines were imposed on others and excessive amounts of goods were seized when these were not paid, leading to great hardship in some cases.

the aberdeen meeting house

TOM MACDONALD adds some personal reminiscences on the Aberdeen Meeting House

During my long search for the title deeds of our property in Aberdeen, which was ultimately successful, I asked John Selkirk if he would examine some of the old Minute Books now lodged in Register House, Edinburgh, and some of the information he obtained is interesting. In 1932 when the tenant of 100 Crown Street was agitating for repairs to be done to the house, M.M. solemnly resolved not to do any repairs "as it was the intention of Two Months Meeting Trust to sell the property whenever possible". Fortunately this was never proceeded with. I have no information as to when the present Meeting House was built, but a Two Months Meeting Minute of 10th June 1903 records that the Meeting House was opened officially on that date. It was still then referred to as 100 Crown Street and it was only later that the address was changed to number 98. It is thought to be the only purpose built Meeting House in Scotland which is still in use for Quaker Meetings.

The Architect who designed our Meeting House was Dr. William Kelly, well known and respected in Aberdeen. He was an LL.D. of Aberdeen University. I remember him well as he was my Sunday School Teacher when I was about seven years of age. He was a tall man of immense dignity with a walrus moustache and not only did he conduct the Sunday School, but he also played the piano for our hymns and gave a vigorous rendering of "Onward Christian Soldiers".

In our title there are certain important restrictions which Friends would be well to keep in mind for the future. We are prohibited from carrying on any business upon the ground or tanning leather, refining tallow, making candles, soap or glue, slaughtering of cattle, erecting gas works, distilleries or iron foundries, making bricks or tiles (except only for our own private use and not for sale) and in general from employing the premises in any trade whatsoever which would be hurtful, nauseous or noxious to the houses or inhabitants in the neighbourhood.

The Quaker Movement in Aberdeen

ALEXANDER GAMMIE, writing in 1909 on the Aberdeen churches, tells of Robert Barclay in the context of Aberdeen church history.

The Quaker movement spread so rapidly after it first took root in the city that the ministers of Aberdeen began to be considerably alarmed at finding so many, both of the higher as well as lower classes, withdrawing from their communion. This led to the beginning of that prolonged and bitter persecution, surely one of the saddest in the religious life of the city. By calumnies and reproaches poured from the pulpits, the ministers endeavoured to incense the magistrates to suppress the Quakers, and to raise among the ruder and less intelligent section of the people a spirit of indignation and vindictive abuse. Hence it was, we are told, that whenever any of the Quaker persuasion appeared in the streets they were received by the populace with stoning and beating, pulling of the hair, and other lawless abuses, which the magistrates, instead of reproving, too often countenanced. Nor was this all. Richard Rae, one of the preachers of the body, was arrested in 1663, and kept a close prisoner in the Tolbooth of Aberdeen for six months, and this was but the beginning of a long series of similar acts. The following year George Keith was cast into prison, and confined for ten months, and Patrick Livingstone, his fellow preacher, became his fellow-prisoner for seven months. Alexander Jaffray, however, was the chief target for the persecutions of those years. His high social position and the reputation he had held in the eyes of the community, made him appear in the eyes of the ministers the most dangerous of the Quakers, and they directed against him their bitterest assaults. He was imprisoned at Banff for nine months, and subjected to the most persistent persecution in every way, but he remained firm in his adherence to the Quaker position, and was the means of greatly strengthening the cause throughout the whole district.

Notwithstanding all the persecution, the Society of Friends in Aberdeen steadily increased, and added to its ranks such worthy members as David and Robert Barclay of Ury, Alexander and Lilias Skene, Thomas Mercer and Andrew Jaffray. These, along with other Quakers, suffered imprisonment repeatedly and almost continuously till the year 1679. The Barclays of Ury made a notable accession to the ranks. Not only were they of high standing locally, but the family was the means, through Robert Barclay, the theologian, of making the influence of Aberdeen Quakers felt throughout the length and breadth of the movement.

One of Barclay's friends on an occasion of uncommon rudeness lamented that he should be treated so harshly in his old age when he had been so highly honoured by the city in his earlier years. "I find more satisfaction," said Barclay, "as well as honour in being thus insulted for my religious principles than when, a few years ago, it was usual for the magistrates as I passed the city of Aberdeen, to meet me on the road and conduct me to public entertainment in their hall, and then escort me out again, to gain my favour."

Robert Barclay, the younger, who was commonly known as "Barclay the Apologist," was destined to take a prominent and influential part in spreading the Quaker movement in Aberdeen, and in expounding the principles of Quakerism to the world at large. The work which fell to his hands was one of supreme importance. Up to this time the doctrines of the Quakers had never been really formulated, and a man of culture and intellectual power was required for this particular task. Such an one was found in Robert Barclay. Possessed of great natural abilities, he had the further advantage of a thorough educational training. His accomplishments were beyond his years, and when he stood forth among the Quakers as the defender of their faith he was fully equipped in every way, and brought to the task both accurate scholarship and vigorous logic. Of his various works, the "Apology" is the most famous. It was published in 1678 under the title of "Apology for the True Christian Divinity, as the same is held forth and preached by the People called in scorn Quakers." It must have been a source of gratification to the local Quakers of the time - as well as those of to-day - that an Aberdeen man had the honour of being the first theologian of the movement. Yet, while Robert Barclay's theological services were great and memorable, they were not his only claim to the gratitude of his fellow Quakers. He moved in aristocratic circles, was a man of influence at Court, and a trusted friend of Elizabeth, the Princess Palatine. The

Princess, on his behalf, used her influence with the King of England, through her brother Rupert, to secure the release of the imprisoned Quakers, and to save them from further oppression.

The imprisonment of the Quakers in Aberdeen came to an end in 1679. In that year the prison doors were opened, never again to be shut on a member of the Society in the city. Many and bitter had been the persecutions of these early years. At first the old Tolbooth had been crowded with Quaker prisoners until new accommodation had to be sought, and this was found in St. Ninian's Chapel on the Castle Hill. The circumstances under which they were confined were often revolting in cruelty, yet, as has already been pointed out, the movement spread in spite of all oppression. Indeed, the greater the persecution the greater also seemed to be the progress of the cause.

It does not appear that the Quakers had any settled Meeting House in Aberdeen for some considerable time after they first made their appearance in the city in 1662. Perhaps this was largely owing to the persistent persecutions of the period, and it is probable that for a number of years they may have met in the houses of one or other of their own number. The first Meeting House on record was situated on the west side of Guestrow, and, although it is doubtful if the building could be definitely pointed out today, yet "Quaker's Court," which is still in existence, may be regarded as affording some indication of where it stood.

ALEXANDER JAFFRAY

Frequent references to Alexander Jaffray are evidence of his influence on the history of Scottish Friends.

Among the remarkable group of people who formed the first Quaker Meeting in Aberdeen in the 1660's Alexander Jaffray stands out because of his involvement in the political affairs of the day. Born in 1614, he was the son of a prominent local merchant and provost of the city. He in turn served his native city as a bailie and as provost. In the turbulent days of the civil war, he was several times returned as a member of parliament for Aberdeen, both to London and Westminster. Indeed, he was virtually Governor of Northern Scotland during the rebellion led by the Marquis of Huntly. Captured and imprisoned in Pitcaple, he and his brother managed with one other prisoner to make themselves masters of the stronghold and burn it to the ground.

As one of six commissioners, he was sent to Holland to negotiate with the exiled Charles II and was instrumental in securing his agreement to recognise the National Covenant in Scotland. Jaffray afterwards regretted that he had been instrumental in persuading the king to go against his conscience in assenting to the document. As a combatant in the battle of Dunbar, where the Scots were defeated by Cromwell, Jaffray was wounded and captured. This brought him into contact with Cromwell, whose views on religious tolerance made a deep impression on him. He became increasingly wearied by the exclusivist claims of the Scottish Presbyterianists, and his *Diary*, part of which was rediscovered in a farmhouse loft in 1827 by John Barclay, who subsequently edited it, records a longing for a pure and uncluttered form of worship. He relied increasingly on private meditation and with a group of friends was involved in an attempt to recapture the idea of the Eucharist as a simple meal.

Under Cromwell's patronage, he became Director of the Chancellory for Scotland. On Charles II's restoration to the throne, he was imprisoned but released on the grounds of ill health in 1661. He retired to Aberdeen, but the preaching tour of William Dewsbury to Scotland meant that his last years were to be full of incident. Dewsbury's preaching persuaded him to join the local group of Friends. He set up a meeting near Aberdeen at Kinmuck, where the old meeting house still exists.

The loss of such a prominent citizen to the Quaker movement incensed an already hostile establishment and Jaffray was ordered to remain in his own house and hold no meetings there. When he refused, he was confined to jail in Banff for over nine months. The experience finally broke his health and the remainder of his life was spent quietly at Kingswells until his death in 1673.

Hugh Pyper

Whittier on Barclay

One day, while Barclay was being insulted while riding in Aberdeen, an old comrade, with soldiers under his command, offered to disperse the crowd, but Barclay would not allow him to use force.

Whittier refers to the incident thus:

Up the streets of Aberdeen,
By the Kirk and College Green,
　　Rode the Laird of Ury.
Close behind him, close beside,
Foul of mouth and evil eyed,
　　Pressed the mob in fury.
Yet with calm and stately mein,
Up the streets of Aberdeen
　　Came he slowly riding;
And to all he saw and heard
Answering not a bitter world,
　　Turning not for chiding.

ROBERT BARCLAY

DELIA SEAGER gives some details of Robert Barclay's life which may be unfamiliar to Friends from south of the Border.

Robert Barclay's life had many similarities to that of William Penn, although he became a prominent theologian rather than a legal reformer. His mother was a Gordon and a grand-daughter of the Earl of Sutherland; Robert was born at Gordonstoun and not at Ury House, on the Barclay's estate near Stonehaven. His father was a distinguished cavalry officer in the Covenanting army and was an M.P. in two of Cromwell's parliaments.

Robert's education was surprising to say the least. He was brought up as a strict Calvinist and then sent to the Scots Theological College in Paris, which was Roman Catholic. His uncle, also called Robert Barclay, was on the staff there, which may explain this change of course. When he was 15 he returned to Scotland in answer to his mother's dying wish.

To put events in their historical perspective - Robert was born in 1648 just at the time when George Fox was beginning to gather together the nucleus of the early Society of Friends, and a year before Charles I was executed after several years of Cromwellian rule. When Robert returned to Scotland from Paris in 1663, Charles II had been on the throne for three years, and in the previous year the 'Quaker Act' had been passed, making it illegal for more than five persons to worship together except according to the practices of the Anglican Church. Enormous fines were imposed for the contravention of this Act. In Scotland, an Act of 1663 which was directed against the Covenanters, caused Friends in Scotland to be persecuted; especially those in Aberdeen.

Following the restoration of the Monarchy, problems for the Barclay family culminated, in 1665, with David Barclay (Robert's father) being arrested and imprisoned in Edinburgh for being on the wrong political side. There he met a Quaker, John Swinton, who was a fellow-prisoner. As a result of their conversations David joined the Society. When Robert visited his father in prison he also became "convinced" after meeting John Swinton.

In 1670 Robert married Christian Molleson, who was a daughter of Gilbert and Margaret molleson, some of the first Friends in Aberdeen. This marriage caused a local scandal because it was carried out not by an ordained minister but according to the practice of the Society of Friends. Presumably non-Friends regarded them as not being married at all. Their descendants included many influential people in Britain and America such as the Barclays (banking) and the Gurneys (Elizabeth Fry's family).

Robert Barclay wrote his famous *Apology* when he was 27 - an account of the truth as Quakers saw it, and still do. He was imprisoned several times in Aberdeen in the Tolbooth, the worst period being during the cold winter of 1677 when he wrote the *Treatise on Universal Love*. In this same year he joined three other eminent Friends, George Fox, William Penn and George Keith (who helped him write the Latin version of the *Apology*), and they went as a team to Holland. Another notable event in his life was the 'Disputation' he had with four scholars from Marischal College, when he came out victorious, if that is the right word!

This even-tempered, cheerful and pleasant man died of a fever in 1690 at the age of 42, just before George Fox himself, and thus the Society lost one of its greatest sources of inspiration.

> *Lilias Skene, a Quaker and contemporary of Robert Barclay, was Aberdeen's first poetess.*

The darkest houre

The darkest houre is ever nearest day;
And tryallis deep for mercies great make way,
When powers of darnkess, hell, and death assaille,
When hope is gone, and human help doth faille,
The Lord is neare, his present help appeares,
Gives secret strength, our doore of error cleares.

KINMUCK - A SAFE REFUGE FROM PERSECUTION

Nowadays Kinmuck is known only as a small village with a few houses. Yet at one time it held the largest community of Quakers in Scotland, and was one of the most northerly meeting places.

They were reviled and persecuted for their beliefs. But here in this remote spot on the slopes of Blair Hussey at Kinmuck, they were safe. Here they could meet in freedom.

The men and women who huddled round the speaker were soberly dressed - the women in poke bonnets and long, plain dresses, the men in grey broadcloth. They hung on the words of Patrick Livingstone of Montrose, one of the followers of George Fox, the founder of Quakerism.

From this small beginning, a colony of Quakers settled in Kinmuck in the years to come. In this quiet little back-water in the shadow of Brimmond Hill, they sought and found refuge from the religious persecution of the outside world.

The Quakers really became established in Kinmuck in 1680 when a piece of land known as Allan's Croft was granted to a schoolmaster, John Robertson, who founded in Kinmuck the first Quaker school in the country.

He taught 'the Latin toung and other commendable learning' and it appears that 'several Considerable people of the World have sent their children thereto: highly commending their profiting therein beyond their own schools'.

But where was the actual school? That is the question which has puzzled many people over the years.

It has always been assumed that Mr. Robertson's school was either in a small croft house on Allan's Croft where he lived with his family or on some other site in Kinmuck which had not been recorded.

When the Rev. Dr. Christopher Armstrong moved into the former Friends' Meeting House in 1967, he wasn't satisfied and his researchings led him to the conclusion that the Meeting House itself goes back to 1680.

In two articles, one printed in Bennachie Again, the other in a 1974 Aberdeen University Review, he documents the evidence. He

Kinmuck Meeting House

contends that when the Friends bought Allan's Croft as a home for the schoolmaster, they also leased a plot of land opposite from the laird of Drum on which to site the purpose-built Kinmuck Meeting House and school .

Both the Meeting House and Allan's Croft, now Bankhead, the home of Robert Cruickshank and his wife, were totally reconstructed in 1832.

The outwardly plain and unpretentious Meeting House still stands today, a B-listed building and one which Dr. Armstrong and his wife, who now live in Hereford, most certainly saved from falling into ruin.

Friends' Cottage, as it is now known, incorporates the 'but and ben' where the caretakers once lived, the long low building which provided stabling for the Quakers' horses - the Loupin' Stane is preserved by the entrance - and the Meeting House itself, unexpectedly stunning in its simplicity. It makes a home of character, a happy, peaceful place.

Some features, says Mrs. Ann Beasley, the present owner, must be carefully preserved - the original fireplace with its massive chimney, making the high-ceilinged room impossible to heat, the minister's gallery and a framed marriage certificate dated 1862, bearing the signatures of all those who attended the ceremony.

Dr. Armstrong considers that the Meeting House originally had two floors and assumes that meetings were held on the ground floor, while the school was taught upstairs.

By 1696, Kinmuck was the largest meeting in Scotland. Quakers still make a pilgrimage to Friends' Cottage, but in its day, it was visited by well-known Quakers from all over the country, including Elizabeth Fry, who in 1818 noted that there was a Women's Meeting House here, which lay between the present cottage and the Meeting House.

By this time, the friends had settled into a peaceful and prosperous existence in Kinmuck, relatively free of local prejudice, each man pursuing his own trade. There were cobblers, tailors and blacksmiths, and some worked at the wool mill.

And now every one of them lies buried in the spartan little walled cemetery next to Bankhead, which is all of Kinmuck that still belongs to the Quakers. A notice on the heavy iron gate advises those interested, of Quaker meetings in Aberdeen.

A visit to the burial ground is a moving experience, for the epitaphs on the serried ranks of gravestones are as simple as the lives these men and women led. They believed there should be no distinction in death as in life.

Only the later graves are marked - the early Friends eschewed such ostentation. There are more than 70 plain sandstone memorials, bearing only the name, age and date of death. One curious fact is that Quakers referred to each month by number, believing the names to be of pagan origins.

Here lie the Cruickshanks, who were cattle breeders; the Wighams, who were silk manufacturer; the Brantinghams, a family of hosiers. Here too lies Amos Wigham, farmer in Kinmuck, whom Friends have noted as the first conscientious objector. In 1803, he was fined 'two fat bullocks' for refusing a Charge for the Militia.

One stone marks the grave of a rogue turned penitent, Peter Brownie, a notorious grave-robber. On one occasion he was returning with a medical student from a successful outing to Newhills cemetery. The corpse, wrapped in shawls, was propped up between the pair of them, when it fell from the gig as they neared their destination.

This so unnerved Brownie that he took early retirement, joined the Quakers and even designed a foolproof mortsafe for Kinmuck cemetery, now in the Anatomy Department at Aberdeen University.

Even today Kinmuck, close to Dyce on one side, Inverurie on the other, has escaped the devastating changes which have smothered other communities. 'People who have lived all their lives in Aberdeen don't seem to have heard of Kinmuck', smiled Mrs. Beasley ruefully.

The few new houses that have been built - mill cottages and a farmhouse have recently been converted - do nothing to detract from the character of the place.

You still get the feeling that it belongs to

another time. In a way it does. Legend says that this place was the site of a great battle between the Danes and the Scots.

The lands were part of the Earldom of the Garioch, created by William the Lion and granted by him to his younger brother, David, Earl of Huntingdon. In 1195, Earl David gifted part of this land, including Kinmuck, to the Abbey of Lindores in Fife, so that for almost 400 years, Kinmuck was held by the Church of Rome. After the Reformation, Kinmuck was acquired by Alexander Irvine of Drum.

All the little businesses and trades that kept the Quaker community so occupied have long since disappeared. The little Victorian school on its site opposite the Meeting House has been replaced by a modern house. The shop and post office next to the pub closed more than 10 years ago.

But the pub remains. And its name, Boar's Head, offers us on a plate the meaning of the name Kinmuck. Where there is muck, there are definately pigs, if we are to believe the Gaelic. Pig's head is in essence what Kinmuck means - from ceann meaning 'head' and muc meaning 'pig'.

Maybe pigs once fed on the land round here...where visitors to the very busy pub now bend their elbows...while the Quakers in the little cemetery up the road are probably turning quietly in their graves.

Visiting Kinmuck

TOM MACDONALD helps us to find our way to visit Kinmuck.

Friends visiting Aberdeen may wish to visit the old Quaker Burial Ground at Kinmuck, about 15 miles from the City. It can be reached by the A96 road to **Inverurie**. Turn right after **Blackburn** along the B979, sign-posted **Hatton of Fintray**. After crossing the **River Don**, take the second turning left, sign-posted **Kinmuck** 1 mile. The Burial Ground is on the left. Aberdeen Friends, who maintain the Ground, have placed a notice on the gate.

Next to the Burial Ground is an Inn named The Boar's Head. The landlord, who takes a great interest in Friends, will be glad to provide coffee, tea and sandwiches.

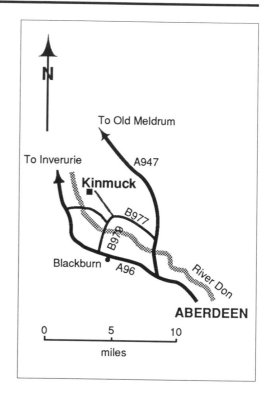

An interesting document has been preserved, signed by 54 Aberdeen Friends, giving us some insight into the life style of Friends about this time. Here are two extracts.

For men they condemned all shooting with guns for game or recreation, or with bow and arrows, hunting with dogs and hawking. In games, dams (draughts), golf and billiards are banned. In dress such details are forbidden as broad ribbands for hat bands, cocking up the side of hats, or vain powdering of wigs or hair, long cravats fringed or speckled, false shoulder pieces, cuffs like shirt sleeves, outside pockets, ranges of useless buttons outside, fancy tops on stockings at the knees, and fancy buckles on the shoes. Coats must be buttoned to the top so as not to display cravats.

The regulations for women are equally stringent. The hair must be put straight back and not set on faces or foreheads. They must wear a plain queff (coif) on their heads without ruffling the front of it. In the hood above, no wires or pasteboard must be used to keep it high, no long laps on hoods and no ruffled neck clothes. The gowns must be plain, without tails to make them sit out behind, and have no low trains. Two and a half ells is the maximum length of scarf allowed, and no coloured plaids may be worn.

16th Fifth mo. '72

Friends being present the meeting continued from 10 forenoon to near 5 in the afternoon. No meeting about affairs.

3rd Tenth mo. '72

Andrew Galloway was desired to order the meeting so with a Barras that Schollars might no Leap over the forms to disturb the meeting as they did most barbarously this day when John Swinton and Robert Barclay were declaring and praying.

THE RED SPOTTED HANDKERCHIEF

Letter from John Hunt Evesham, New Jersey, of date 25.3mo 1786 to John Townsend Philadelphia urging him to desist from wearing a red spotted handkerchief.

Perhaps some of our readers know how this letter came to be preserved in the Register House in Edinburgh. Who was John Hunt? - and what were his links with Scotland?

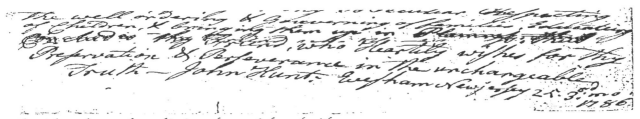

Notwithstanding we have this several years laboured with him and kept him from it I think I should be as much against admitting them kind of Handkerchiefs into my family as ever thee was against the newfangled bonets in thy family or amongst thy children. A Friend a few years ago informed me that he had a large family of children one of which was Dumb, but they were not at a loss to convey their thoughts and meaning to him by signs and motions, the man was an Elder and his wife a Minister and much concerned to keep their children out of the vain customs and fashions of the world, but this dumb lad wanted one of these spotted handkerchiefs and his parents stood against it; at Length there came along a Travelling Friend and he and his Companion both having this kind of handkerchief about their Neck, it so strengthened the Dumb Lad that he began again to Contend with his parents for one, so we may see how these things weaken our hands in bringing up our children in plainness, and if Friends of the foremost rank cannot condescend today by things that burden one another how can we expect our youth will condesend to us; I am fully clear that if thee could, in condescention to thy Friends, lay by thy Red Spotted Handkerchief and get one all of one moderate grave colour it would be a Matter of Great Gladness to very many honest hearted well concerned Friends that are very desirous to bring up their children in Plainness, which we say truth Requires, the more Especially because thy Service is like to be so extensive on our continent as I said before, thy Testimony so peculiar respecting the well ordering and Governing of families, educating of children and bringing them up in plainness. Thus concludes thy Friend, who heartily wishes for thy Preservation and Perseverance in the unchangeable Truth.

John Hunt.
Evesham, New Jersey. 25.3rd. mo. 1786

Friends of Aberdeen were favoured with much good advice, much of which is surely relevant today. These extracts are from a "weighty paper containing severall heads of solid advyces and Counsells to frinds from the half years meeting in Ireland"

[All Friends to be just in their dealings, etc.] that their yea and nay may not be violated but may stand firm as at first when the Lord called us to be a People: and Let their words be few and savory, and not to take Liberty to multiply unsavory talk in their concerns on any acount, but know a bridle, and their words seasoned with grace.

And keep to the plain Languag and train up their children theirin.

And Shun and avoyd unnecessary company Lest any therby be drawn into temptations. And take heed of being overcome with strong drink or tobacco, which many by custome are brought into bondag to the creature. . . .

And that frinds refrain from decking or adorning their rooms with needles things and ther kitchens with flourishing needless pewter and Brass which the mynd that goes from God into the World desires and gets and is never settled nor satisfied.

And that all frinds be carefull that they Jnvolve not themselves in the things of the World. . . .

[All Friends to be diligent in attending week day meetings.]

And that all frinds may depart from meetings in the sense of the Lord's goodnes and meditat theirin: And not Jmediatly after a goodly meeting fall into discourse of Worldly things which is too frequent and seems to be the work of the Enemy that picks out the good seed that was sowed in the meeting.

And in all your men and womens meetings, be solid and grave, refrain all needles discourse. Neither speak above one at a tyme. For if otherwise Jt is neither edifying nor answers the service of the concerns befor you.

[Friends are advised against travelling on First days on their worldly business, whereby they are hindered from attending meetings, besides offending others.]

[Anent Marriage] *The Lord and his Truth to be preferred above all. And let parents on both sides know the mynd of each other about portions befor ther children make any progress in that case of marriag.* [The children are to acquaint their parents and to obtain their consent, before] they make ther mynds known on to the other.

[Friends are advised to keep "a true record" of Births, Marriages, Burials, Wills, etc.]

Eleanor Robertson tells us that her father met this friend (Philip) on a fishing holiday, and kept in touch with him for the rest of his life. He had hoped to expose Philip to the advantages of Quakerism by taking him to a Meeting.

Roger Clark of Street, Somerset, wrote to his brother from Aberdeen on 29 January, 1897, as follows:

"On Saturday a large party of us went to the Pantomime Matinee, but it was a very foolish performance and we left early. On Sunday Philip and I went to Meeting in the morning which was also a very Foolish performance only we did not leave early. Two half crazy women ranted away, one had to be silenced, with much difficulty, and both decamped. Others made long dreary prayers and dry addresses. A stifling heat, a new smart room like a chapel, with vulgar stained windows and coloured texts at the end above the railed platform, and an hour and a half long. I felt sick and faint with mortification, bodily and mental."

Things have changed since then!

Quoted from Quaker Inheritance, 1871 - 1961 *by Percy Lovell, The Bannisdale Press, London, 1970*

DELIA SEAGER gives us some more glimpses of Friends of the past.

After the Second World War there was a drive to clear away what had become slum-dwellings opposite Marischal College. The City architects' fight, supported by the Queen Mother, to save some of these historic but dilapidated buildings has left us with one of Aberdeen's showpieces, Provost Skene's House. But all round it the ancient centre of the town was flattened, to be replaced by the massive concrete and glass edifice of St. Nicholas House. Although it is dwarfed by its young neighbour, Provost Skene's House attracts many visitors, but how many know that if they walked round the side of the mansion and looked at the shrub border against its rear wall, they would be gazing at the site of Quaker Court?

This cul-de-sac running westwards from the old Guestrow, parallel with Broad Street, was where a number of Quakers owned property and where the first Meeting House in Aberdeen was situated in the late seventeenth centuries. It briefly became part of national history in 1746 when the notorious Duke of Cumberland, younger son of George II, was quartered in Provost Skene's House ("Cumberland's Lodging") and requisitioned the Meeting House for use as a mint to pay his crack troops who were pursuing the remnants of the Jacobite army as it fled northwards.

But before this upheaval, and following the fanatical persecution of Quakers in the twenty years before about 1680, there must have been a period of quiet consolidation for Friends in the area. Some picture of life at this time comes to us from three legal documents signed by Mary Bannerman, who lived in one of the houses adjacent to the Meeting House off Guestrow. Her witnesses and executors include Robert Barclay, son of the eminent Quaker theologian, and Alexander Jaffray, son of one of the notable early converts to Quakerism in Aberdeen. Mary Bannerman was the well-to-do widow of George Leslie of Findrassie and by 1706 had lived in her Aberdeen house "for a considerable time". She was putting her affairs in order in anticipation of her death, but despite this was obviously travelling about the countryside. She wished to be buried in the Friends burial ground in Gallowgate, which earlier had suffered many attacks from the authorities. However, she did not want to cause inconvenience to Friends if she died while away from home; in that case she specified that she should be buried at Ury (the Barclay estate near Stonehaven), or at Kinmuck, a few miles north-west of Aberdeen, or at Aquhorthies, near Oldmeldrum. The burial grounds at Kinmuck and Ury (a private one) are still in existence, but the earliest graves have no headstones, in the manner of early Friends.

A no-fuss-and-bother lady, she seems to have had doubts about her (non-Quaker) relations being of the same mind when it came to arrangements for her funeral, as part of a document dated "Second day of the first month (old March) One Thousand and seven hundred and four years" indicates:
"It having pleased the Lord in his Great mercie to bring me to a Sence and knowledge of his blessed and precious Truth called Quakerisme (in derision) which I have owned and proffessed many years, and wherein I hope to dye and lay down my head in peace with the Lord my God in and thurrow his Dear Son Jesus Christ my alone Saveour and Redeemer. I order that after my death my body is to be taken care of and wrapped in plain Gravecloaths as the manner of Friends of the Truth is, by the care of Women friends of the Meeting where I lay down the Body, and my Relations without any manner of vain superfluous attire unsuitable to my profession. And that it be put in a plain Coffine without any mulloring, Carving or Collouring. And that no mortcloath of any collour be put thereupon and that it be carried to the head of Gallowgate at Aberdeine if I dye there or near to it and that there be no mourning habites nor Crapes used by any of my Relations, as they would wish to show their Last respects to me in fulfilling my last will."

Then, two and a half years later (5th November, 1706), she gives a picture of some of the furnishings of her house:

"I appoint my Executors to deliver to John Glenny at the Meeting at Lethenty[1] ane compleit bedding of cloathes, viz. a feather bed, ane bolster, two pillows, two pairs of plaides and a faike, a pair of sheets, a Covering with hangings about the bedd, ane Chamber pot, ane little table, two Chaires covered with red Leather, one Armed and the other plaine, and also I hereby declair that there are Eight wandscott chairs in the hall belonging to Findrassie which must be returned to him."[2]

The last document, dated 3rd January 1712, appoints four Trustees to dispose of the rent of her "tenement and garden" in Guestrow ("Gaste Raw"); it shows her concern for education and the welfare of others. The Trustees are given power "to settle and secure the said tenement and garden from time to time in any person's name they think fit, being a Member of the Monthly Meeting of the people called Quakers in Aberdeen, and to uplift the yearly maills and duties thereof yearly and termly". This money was to be used for the relief of poor Friends within the Monthly Meeting. At each Monthly Meeting the condition of the poor was to be carefully considered so "that they may be relieved according to their necessities". She also deals with a bond for 100 merks Scots money, whose annual income was to be paid to the Mistress of the Women's School in Aberdeen as part of her annual salary. (This school was only short-lived)

Maybe in time it will be possible to track down more information about the life and times of Mary Bannerman, but some records of the period are damaged or missing. When was she born, and married, and when and where was she buried? There was a long-standing legend that her grave was in her back garden, but when it eventually came to be opened this century, the supposed coffin was found to be a horse trough. She might have enjoyed the joke!

1. *Lethenty is near Fyvie and had an active Meeting*

2. *Findrassie was her husband's home, and presumably "him" refers to a relative then owning it.*

EARLY 20Th CENTURY ABERDEEN FRIENDS

This is another extract from Alexander Gammie's paper on the churches of Aberdeen

From the figures which have been kept, it would appear that there had never been a very large Meeting in Aberdeen - at least since the days of the persecution. In 1790 there were 44 members; in 1830 there were 28; and in 1868 there is a list of 28 members and 13 attenders. Within more recent years, and in the present day, there has been but little variation in the numbers. What the Society in Aberdeen may lack in numerical strength is, however, largely compensated for by the loyalty to the cause of those who are in full membership, and by the faithfulness with which they uphold the principles of the body. They occupy a place quite unique in the religious life of the city, and by their quiet, unobtrusive, yet strong attachment to their own position, they commend themselves to their brethren of other persuasions, and to the community generally. The days of persecution are long past, and it would be difficult to find any religious sect more highly esteemed by the ministers and churches in Aberdeen to-day than the once-oppressed Quakers. The distinctive dress they wore in former generations has almost entirely disappeared from the streets of the city, their peculiar forms of speech are seldom heard. They may appear less picturesque in the public eye, but they still raise their testimony for something distinctive, both in life and doctrine.

Aberdeen Friends Today

Quaker history is still in the making. Here, four of our Aberdeen Friends show us some of the ways in which they are meeting the needs of the present day, and preparing themselves for the challenges of the future.

Aberdeen Friends are very active in many different avenues of service in the local community individually, but have not worked collectively as a general rule.

For example, four Friends have been visitors at Aberdeen and Peterhead prisons, usually singly, though once they had a Christmas service with three prisoners who had asked for Quaker visitors.

As an example of individual concern, one Friend escorted a teenage group, 24 of them, from London via Paris to Geneva on two occasions for their fortnight's study of the United Nations (ECOSOC).

Another Friend has been busy with others in the College of Education recently, editing a very attractive set of books, delightfully illustrated, for use in schools, named "Learning through Living".

Anne Benzie

Four years ago two members of Aberdeen Meeting started attending the Clinical Theology Association's course in Aberdeen. Since then another four members and attenders in the Monthly Meeting have been participants. Originally the course was planned to provide counselling training for clergy but now it also caters for a considerable number of lay people. It is concerned with human relationships, pastoral care and counselling and "is designed to enable those who work with people to improve their capacity to respond helpfully to others, and to identify areas within themselves which limit their own helpfulness."

The emphasis on personal growth and the value of our own experience probably makes the form of the course particularly attractive to Quakers. In fact, we have sometimes been able to act as a bridge between the basically Anglican theology underlying Clinical Theology and the views of group members who have no stated faith.

Having said this though, the course is about people and how they react to life's situations.

The simple exercises, which are an integral part of the syllabus, helped us to value the qualities of other group members (and, hopefully, our own), to realise that we can share difficulties without being harmed, and to respect one another. Perhaps this simply says that we have learned more about our common humanity. Almost certainly we have found that being open to change in our lives can be painful but that it brings its rewards in increased freedom and openness to others. As well as leading to personal growth the course has been of great value to those of us who are involved in any form of counselling, whether formally or informally in our daily lives.

Delia Seager

The Meeting has grown over the last thirty years, and this continuing trend of growth was brought home to me in a curious way - when we went to Zimbabwe in 1983 and joined the Meeting in Harare, we had a sense of the two meetings, Harare and Aberdeen being of much the same size and vitality. But when we came back to Aberdeen in 1986, we came into what felt like an altogether bigger meeting - more at meetings for worship, more offices and more Friends to share them around. Added to that, Aberdeen PM was the dominant part of the North of Scotland MM when we left, with Friends elsewhere either scattered or in one or two very small groupings, we came back to a sense of vital activity throughout the N.E. area - with recognised meetings in Moray and Nairn, Inverness (investing in developing its own meeting house), Orkney and Shetland. Barclay and other early North-East Friends would be proud of us - if such a vice is compatible with Quaker weightiness!

Nigel Dower

Our second child was stillborn on 30th May 1983. It was a devastating experience, and we much appreciated the support of our friends and relatives. However, the ability to share our feelings with two friends, each of whom had lost a child, gave me the opportunity to share all sorts of doubts that I had felt unable to express to others. Bereavement can be a bewildering experience, and there was some reassurance that these anxieties were part of the process of grieving for a child.

With the help of the national Stillbirth And Neonatal Death Society (SANDS) I made contact with other bereaved parents locally. We held an Open Meeting in October '84 and our group, called Daybreak, came into being - "Daybreak" - because we felt we wanted to give the feeling that there could be a new dawn, despite the despair.

The group has had its ups and downs but the maternity hospital Social Work Department have kept a continuing interest. We have circulated our name through the libraries, and the local Voluntary Services directory. As well as responding to the individual parents who contact us we have spoken to the the Maternity Hospital about how they manage patients who suffer stillbirth, and we presented the labour ward with a Moses basket so that those precious few photographs, which are often all that are left to treasure, can be less clinical.

Barbara Potter

ChE FIRST QUAKER IN SHETLANO

There are, of course, Friends living and meeting much further north than Aberdeen. North of Scotland MM has Meetings in Moray and Nairn, Inverness and the islands of Orkney and Shetland. Today we can leave Aberdeen at 18.00 hours and arrive in Shetland in time for breakfast.

There are now about 25 Friends in the islands with from 7 to10 attending local Meetings.

This year I had the privilege of meeting a Quaker lady from London who was retracing, as far as possible, the steps of her ancestor Sarah Squire, the first Quaker to set foot in these islands. That was in the summer of the year 1835 and her descendant's intention was to follow out this journey at the same time of year, visiting all the places mentioned in Sarah's carefully documented journal of her experiences.

Reading the account of this early Quaker certainly makes one realise that 'women's lib' is not a prerogative of recent years. At the time of her Shetland journey Sarah was 53 years old and the mother of eight children. Leaving husband and family behind she set out on a two month tour of Shetland to be followed by a further month in Orkney. In those days this was an undertaking which we can hardly picture indeed.

This simple document of facts is a revelation. The sea voyage from Leith to Lerwick on a sailing ship called the Norna took six whole days, often in most unfavourable conditions.

Although the month was June, when we expect better things, the year 1835 happened to be an exceptionally poor summer. The rough weather and the state of the country would have daunted any but the most determined, but they did not deter Sarah whose mission it was to carry her message through these islands.

Riding side-saddle in her voluminous skirts this middle-aged lady climbed hills 'steep as the side of a house' as she says in her diary. There were no roads in Shetland then apart from a short stretch in Lerwick itself. The country was a maze of bog and marshland, the tracks round the coastline often precipitous. The best hope of progress was to rely on the ponies with their instinctive knowledge of where it was safe to tread.

Nothing discouraged this remarkable woman from making her way to the most remote places. Accompanied by a female companion and two guides she traversed the islands as far north as Unst. The more clement parts south of Cunningsburgh she left for others, perhaps less venturesome, to negotiate.

89

She visited the island of Papa Stour where she stayed with Gideon Henderson in the house where Lindsay, the prisoner of Papa Stour, was held captive for 26 years. At the time of Sarah's visit, this unfortunate man was shortly to be released. That is a story in itself, only mentioned in passing here.

Wherever they went Sarah and her party stayed with the best-known families who obviously provided them with ponies and boats. Everywhere she lodged Sarah praises the hospitality of her hosts and the welcome with which they were greeted. Occasionally, as in Sandness, she writes that decent accommodation could not be found, the sanitary arrangements not being up to her standard. One cannot help wondering what sort of sanitation there was anywhere in Shetland in 1835.

Wherever they lodged, Sarah made that her centre for holding meetings and it is amazing how many people gathered together. In Fetlar where the present population is less than 100 Sarah reports a congregation of 300 people at her meeting. From Reawick, where she stayed with the merchant James Garriock, Sarah crossed the voe to Leans, a tiny place with few houses and no church, where she addressed a gathering of 100 eager listeners. She also held meetings in far more isolated places, going as far north as Fethaland, where a small colony of fishermen lived during the summer months.

As there was no suitable saddle for her, Sarah was obliged to walk the three miles of very rough going from Isbister to this most northerly point of the Shetland mainland, but that again proved no obstacle to her carrying the message to those fishermen. In that solitary spot she spoke to a substantial gathering of some 100 souls. Nowadays few people, mainly bird-watchers, make their way to those derelict dwellings. There the chance visitor may stop to rest on the old house walls and wonder who could have lived there. In Sarah's day there was real life in Fethaland.

There are not many buildings left standing where she is known to have spoken. In Hillswick and Ollaberry the old churches have long been replaced, but in North Roe, where the church built in 1828 is still intact, Sarah did actually hold a meeting. She also visited Lunna and Busta House which she must have found quite luxurious compared with some of her accommodation.

The account of the whole incredible journey has been preserved in Sarah's own journal which she must have written up day by day in her fine neat handwriting. It is hoped that this will be published in book form with the necessary elucidations and comments by her descendant who has interested herself in the pilgrimage. If there is anybody in Shetland who has any further knowledge of this first Quaker mission it would be of interest in compiling the story of Sarah Squire's tour.

How many Quakers there are at present in Shetland I do not know. They are scattered and have little opportunity of assembling together. In any case the account of Sarah's journey will be of considerable interest to many others concerned with Shetland history in the early nineteenth century.

M. Bowden

School of Aberdeen, 1682

One fancies from the following minute of the Quarterly Meeting, Forth Month, 1682, that the school established at Aberdeen must have been of a somewhat humble character:

"As to the provision for the School of Aberdene frinds concluds That the former provision (annual salary) for Margaret Ker be continued (ie six bolls of meill and two bolls bear and house room in the Meeting House) And have also found their hearts open to give her some further particular encouragement for the year till the school increase. Also men frinds thinks That Lillias Skene and Isobel Gerard speak to Margaret Ker That she may take some care to accomplish herself in arithmetic and writting for the education of the children."

Orkney Meeting

A Friend from Orkney extends a welcome to visitors.

Friends now meet in Ornkey on 2nd and 4th Sundays moving amongst eight households during the year. One family drives 40 miles (wind and tide permitting) when Meeting for Worship is in Stromness, but for most of us the drive varies between 5 and 25 miles. On Easter Sunday I fitted 14 chairs into my sitting room and all were needed. Our Children's Meeting now consists of six school-age junior Friends and we have four Young Friends of senior school and college age. Several have attended Northern Friends Summer School and JYM and we are pleased at the prospect of a Northern Friends Senior Conference for 17+ in 1989. For several years Children's Meeting has been in touch with the Meeting at Doylestown PA (USA) and we recently welcomed Jacob Stone from Doylestown on a brief visit to see Orkney (in blizzards) and Orkney Friends and to bring gifts and greetings from the children.

We are almost all 'ferry-loupers', in comers to a long-established traditional island community where the churches are vigorous and supportive and where family networks still provide a caring community. But we do take part in island life: attender and Friend households alike serve or have served the community both on a voluntary and a career basis in health care, care of the elderly and handicapped, in schools, farming, as air port fireman and Loganair pilot, as well as taking part in and serving on committees of special interest groups - weaving, Field Club, museum and music and Amnesty International. Some of us attend the local church when there is no Meeting for Worship: we take part, when invited, in the World Day of Prayer and give talks to the Women's Guilds (kirk) and even (once) to the Ministers' Fraternal.

We welcome visitors to Orkney and in 1988 John Noble and Andrew Clark visited us from Friends House. Earlier in the year Friends brought us one of the panels of the Quaker Tapestry so that we could work on it. Our children had contributed sketches, parts of which were included.

Elsie Taylor

Borders Friends

*LINKS BETWEEN
ABERDEEN AND
THE BORDERS*

*It may surprise our
readers to learn that
the Borders , the most
recent PM to be
established in
Scotland, had close
links with Aberdeen in
the past. These notes
have been prepared by
Lewis Wigham from
material written by
Gray Wallis and
Norman Ferguson.
We wish Borders
Friends well for this
new phase in their
history.*

An early reference to Friends in the Borders is made in the minutes of an Adjourned Meeting held at Aberdeen 19:10:1786 (Minute Book N1):

"Following minutes having been read twice are agreed to this Meeting. On solidly considering the answers to the Queries, and the low state of the several Meetings with the small number of Friends, constituting Aberdeen and Kelso Monthly Meeting it is agreed that Aberdeen be joined with Kinmuck and Old Meldrum Monthly Meetings under the name of Aberdeen Monthly Meeting, and to comprehend all the particular Meetings of Friends situated North of the River Tay.

"Also that Edinburgh and Kelso be in like manner joined under the name of Edinburgh Monthly Meeting, and to comprehend such Meetings and Friends as are on the south side of the River Tay not joined to any other Meeting."

In 1821, a Friends Meeting House was acquired in Buccleuch Street, Hawick. Meetings were held there until 1844. It was used as a hospital during Hawick's second cholera epidemic, in 1847. After being let as a school, the building was sold in 1866. Most of the Friends in Hawick consisted of the families of William Wilson and William Watson who were leading woollen manufacturers.

In 1903, James Glenny and his wife were Friends in Hawick, attending General Meeting and other Meetings in Edinburgh, but worshipping at East Barn, now Unity, Church every Sunday.

Prior to 1957, Borders Friends arranged occasional Meetings in Hawick. There were five Friends: Gray Wallis, Joanna Henderson and Nancy Dickie all of Hawick; and Phyllis Alletson and Marjorie Dolan both of Jedburgh.

In 1958, the first Meeting was held at The Grove, Denhholm, the home of Rosemary and Norman Ferguson. Meetings were then held regularly almost every month, mainly at The Grove and occasionally at other Friends' homes.

Between 1957 and 1967, four large gatherings were held with guest speakers. Friends attended from Edinburgh, Glasgow, Carlisle and Newcastle. Two were in Minto House, a private school near Denholm, one in Minto Village and one in the Episcopal Church Room at Jedburgh.

In 1967, the Fergusons moved away from Denholm and Gray Wallis had already died. Attendance was falling and Meetings were held on the first Sunday of the month in different Friends' homes.

Around 1970, Meetings were held on the first and third Sundays of the month in Darnick Village Hall. In 1975 these twice monthly Meetings were held at the home of Dorothy Treadway, Earlston.

In 1988, Dorothy Treadway was unable to house a growing Meeting that had begun to meet weekly. The venue thus became The Abbey Row Community Centre, Kelso.

On the fifth of March, 1989, Borders Recognised Meeting agreed upon a minute requesting that South East Scotland Monthly Meeting award them status as a Preparative Meeting. This minute was considered by the Monthly Meeting which was held at Peebles on March 18th 1989, and that Meeting established Borders' Friends as a Preparative Meeting. It had fluctuated and moved from place to place over the past 30 years but has now settled in Kelso. "...We have been reminded that Kelso has a very early mention in Quaker records. There are 17 members on the Monthly Meeting list at present attending Borders Recognised Meetings. Arrangements are well established with regard to regular Meetings, and to the care of children and young people. Meeting for Worship is already being held weekly in Kelso and at regular though less frequent intervals in Peebles and Innerleithan. Borders Meeting see the establishment of a Preparative Meeting as an important way of growing and developing Quaker witness in the Borders. We welcome this initiative of Borders Friends and agree to establish Borders Preparative Meeting..."

Epilogue

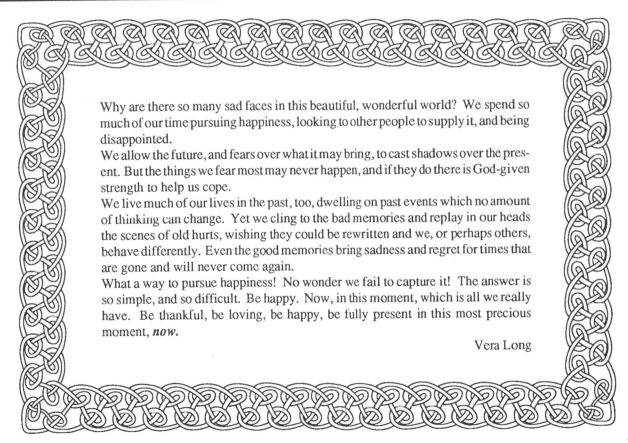

Why are there so many sad faces in this beautiful, wonderful world? We spend so much of our time pursuing happiness, looking to other people to supply it, and being disappointed.

We allow the future, and fears over what it may bring, to cast shadows over the present. But the things we fear most may never happen, and if they do there is God-given strength to help us cope.

We live much of our lives in the past, too, dwelling on past events which no amount of thinking can change. Yet we cling to the bad memories and replay in our heads the scenes of old hurts, wishing they could be rewritten and we, or perhaps others, behave differently. Even the good memories bring sadness and regret for times that are gone and will never come again.

What a way to pursue happiness! No wonder we fail to capture it! The answer is so simple, and so difficult. Be happy. Now, in this moment, which is all we really have. Be thankful, be loving, be happy, be fully present in this most precious moment, *now.*

Vera Long

References

Alexander Gammie	Extract from his Chapter on "The Society of Friends (or Quakers) in "The Churches of Aberdeen" published in 1909.
John Hunt	Letter now in the Register House, Edinburgh, made available by courtesy of Anne P. Young and reproduced by kind persmission of Scottish Records Office Ref CH10/3/97
Rev. John Torrance	Extract from a paper given to the Banff Field Club on 20 Nov 1936
Records of Aberdeen YM 1692	"Solid Advyces and Counsells"
"The First Quaker in Shetland"	Reproduced with the permission of the Editor of "Shetland Life"
"A Safe Refuge from Persecution"	By Courtesy of the Aberdeen Evening Express

The Line Drawings

Kinmuck Meeting House	From an original watercolour in Aberdeen Meeting House
Quiet Times	From an original watercolour by Kathleen Laurie
Moving to Scotland	Helen Tyas
A Bygone World	Marlène Walker-Colward
Living in the Borders, The Rugged Road and Peace House	Anne Woolgrove